Sports Illustrated

FENWAY

A FASCINATING FIRST CENTURY

Sports Illustrated BOOKS

FITTINGLY DESCRIBED AS A
precious gem of a ballpark,
Fenway has, against all odds,
remained fixed in precisely the
same setting for 100 years.
Photograph by JEAN-PIERRE LESCOURRET

Sports Illustrated

FENWAY

A FASCINATING FIRST CENTURY

Sports Illustrated BOOKS

Introduction
THE BALLPARK THAT WOULDN'T DIE *Fenway has survived all attempts to eradicate it* BY STEVE RUSHIN 6

A History in Brief
A BELOVED AND IRREGULAR PLACE *Born quirky, Fenway Park remains a baseball haven* BY TOM VERDUCCI ... 10

The Green Monster
THE POWER OF THE WALL *Fenway's leftfield icon once bedeviled the Red Sox* BY JACK MANN 24

THE FENWAY TIMELINE

Little Fenways
FENWAY IN FACSIMILE *The cherished old ballpark has spawned a host of inspired re-creations* 190

The Fenway 100
FAVORITE FACTOIDS *Of a century's worth of tidbits about Fenway, these are the best* BY DAVID SABINO 194

DAVID BAUER
Editor

HOFFMAN NOLI DESIGN
Art Direction

CRISTINA SCALET
Photo Editor

KEVIN KERR
Copy Editor

STEFANIE KAUFMAN
Project Manager

DAVID SABINO
Associate Editor

JOSH DENKIN
Designer

RYAN HATCH
Reporter

IN THE HOURS LEADING UP TO his last game before rejoining the Marines, in Korea in the spring of '52, Ted Williams took a solitary stroll through the quiet Fenway Park stands.
Photograph by LEONARD MCCOMBE

THE BALLPARK THAT WOULDN'T DIE

Almost from its birth, Fenway Park has been besieged by frightful attempts to eradicate it, only to survive them all

BY STEVE RUSHIN

LIKE THE PARK ITSELF, THE DENTED surface of the Green Monster at Fenway has taken a beating over the years, which has only enhanced its charm.

WHEN A RETIRED THEATER MANAGER NAMED ABRAHAM STOKER EXPIRED IN ENGLAND AT AGE 64, AFTER A SERIES OF STROKES, THE INTERNATIONAL NEWS REPORTS THAT HE WAS DEAD AND GONE WEREN'T ENTIRELY ACCURATE. STOKER WAS DEAD, CERTAINLY, BUT NOT GONE. OR RATHER GONE, BUT NOT DEAD.

For Bram Stoker had already staked (if you will) his claim to immortality, creating a deathless count from the Carpathian Mountains in an 1897 novel called *The Un-Dead*, a title that was changed on the eve of publication to *Dracula*. And though Bram Stoker, through Count Dracula, never really died, he was emphatically declared dead at No. 26 St. George's Square, London, on April 20, 1912, the curtain ringing down on one celebrated existence just as it was rising on another.

For that debut, we have to cross the Atlantic—not an easy task on April 20, 1912, as passengers steaming for New York aboard the SS *Bremen* would attest. In the frigid waters that day they reported "many piteous sights," including three lifeless figures clinging to a single steamer chair; empty life rings afloat in the water; and the stiffened body of a woman in a nightdress, baby still clasped to her breast.

All had been passengers on the RMS *Titanic*, which struck an iceberg six days earlier en route to New York. If not for that tragedy, the *Titanic* would have launched its return voyage to England that very day—at noon on April 20, 1912—an exceedingly inauspicious date to be setting out on a long journey.

The only baseball player to embark on a major league career that day—the unfortunate Benny Kauff, who debuted for the New York Highlanders—would be banned from the game for life by commissioner Kenesaw Mountain Landis, for alleged ties to an auto theft ring. Kauff would never be reinstated to the game, despite his unambiguous acquittal in a court of law.

YOU COULD SAY THAT FENWAY was born under a bad sign—indeed, more than one—as Count Dracula and the ill-fated "Titanic" attest

JUDGE LANDIS (TOP) CAST
an unwitting shadow on
Fenway's birth, a fire nearly
caused its death, and Tom
Yawkey saved its life.

Two ballparks were born on April 20, 1912, with very different life expectancies. Tiger Stadium opened in Detroit, initially named Navin Field, and would survive into a beautiful blue-rinsed old age, finally passing after 87 years in a kind of crumbling grandeur.

The other park born that day, would not, it appeared, be so lucky. Malevolent forces were trying to do away with the fledgling Fenway Park in Boston as early as October of 1918, only six years after it opened.

America was gripped by a new austerity following its entry into World War I when the owner of the Boston Red Sox, Harry Frazee, joined manager Ed Barrow in inspecting Braves Field only weeks after the Sox had won the 1918 World Series. Frazee was considering sharing that park with the National League's Boston Braves. Maintaining two ballparks in Boston, for limited summertime use, seemed "out of harmony with the systems of efficiency in vogue at present," as the *Boston Daily Globe* put it that Halloween, an apposite date for this horror-born ballpark near Kenmore Square.

In the end, Frazee did nothing quite so karma-fraught as abandoning Fenway, and made do instead with selling Babe Ruth to the Yankees.

When the Great War could not kill Fenway, Mother Nature took a stab. Three separate fires in 1926 consumed the wooden bleachers that ran along Fenway's leftfield line. The park would be rebuilt—and refurbished, and reconfigured, for the rest of the 20th century—but by the end of the millennium, when Tiger Stadium closed in 1999, Fenway Park was finally declared unfixable.

"It would be easier to straighten the Leaning Tower of Pisa," Red Sox owner John Harrington said that season, when the park hosted its valedictory All-Star Game, which in turn hosted Fenway's greatest star, Ted Williams, who later would himself prove remarkably resistant to conventional modes of death.

Thirteen years later, the Leaning Tower still leans in Pisa, and Fenway Park in Boston remains upright, flourishing in its 100th year, impossible to kill by fire, by old age or even by its own hand. As ballparks go, it is The Un-Dead, though devotion to it has seldom been undying.

BY THE TIME TOM YAWKEY PURCHASED the Red Sox, for $1.2 million in 1933, the ballpark was already familiar with near-death experiences, and was sinking into a deep decrepitude at age 21. Yawkey set about rebuilding Fenway

entirely that winter, but in the course of doing so—on Jan. 5, 1934—another fire spread from a building across the street and burned the ballpark for five hours. The new grandstand in leftfield was ravaged, as were the centerfield bleachers, requiring $575,000 in repairs and the construction of steel-and-concrete replacements. The park's walls were likewise fireproofed in tin and concrete, including the new leftfield wall, built to a height of 37 feet. Tom Yawkey had, albeit unwittingly, done what Bram Stoker did 37 years earlier: he had created a timeless monster.

Only nobody called it that yet. The wall wouldn't be painted until 1947, giving birth to its nickname, the Green Monster, a mythological creature from some gothic novel. Every decade for the next half century, Fenway Park would be stalked by baying mobs—of real-estate developers, government officials and even its own proprietors—bearing metaphorical torches and pitchforks, wanting to do away with the beast. That same year, 1947, seven light towers were installed, the first step in Fenway becoming, like Stoker's count, a largely nocturnal creature, often unloved and forever under siege.

And so what nature could not achieve with fire, man set out to do. The willful demolition of Fenway Park was being proposed since at least its early middle age. In 1958, when the Giants and Dodgers left New York in part for want of parking near their urban ballparks, the president of the Metropolitan Coal Company in Boston proposed to build a domed "dream stadium, [an] ultra-modern sports palace" on Route 1 in Norwood, Mass. The financial backers of this privately funded Xanadu would move ahead only if the Red Sox agreed to serve as tenants in this stately pleasure dome.

Had the dream come to pass, Ted Williams would have ended his career not in "a lyric little bandbox of a ballpark," as John Updike famously described Fenway in 1960, but beneath a synthetic sky, spectators ensconced in $5,000-a-year "delux boxes," in a suburban redoubt replete with a 100-tee driving range and "bowling alleys with glassed-in nurseries" for "pin-minded mothers."

Think of Williams, in his final at bat, hitting a home run and refusing to do what the stadium could—which is to say, doff its cap. For this was to have been a retractable-roofed Red Sox park, to replace the obsolescent Fenway, which was 48 years old and with scant parking, and thus doomed in the automotive utopia of Eisenhower's America, with its carhops and drive-ins and nascent interstate highways.

THE SOX STAYED, OF COURSE, BUT THE dream of the dome would not die. In the 1960s—the decade in which America resolved to visit the moon—the Greater Boston Stadium Authority planned another dome, suitably space-aged, near South Station. That stadium and an adjacent arena would be home not just to the Sox but also the Patriots, Bruins and Celtics, ridding the city of blighted Fenway and the benighted parquet of Boston Garden with one progressive sweep of the wrecking ball.

The new ballpark would resemble the other state-of-the-art stadia going up in St. Louis, Atlanta, Oakland and Washington, D.C., big round symmetrical quadruplets, multipurpose and multi-parking-spaced, without Monsters or Pesky Poles or hand-operated scoreboards.

In the absence of winning teams, these dream proposals were lovely to contemplate, and so such proclamations were issued—almost exactly—at 10-year intervals. It was in 1969 that the club considered a $40 million proposal to expand Fenway to 50,000 seats by "knocking out the leftfield wall," vanquishing the Monster within the monster, killing the vampire by staking its heart. A decade later, in '79, the Sox made a veiled threat to Boston mayor Kevin White that the club would move to a multiuse stadium in suburban Wilmington.

BY THE LATE 1980S, THE SOX planned a $50 million "revitalization" of Fenway that included a five-deck parking garage. Fenway, built four years after the introduction of the Model T, never had a place to put the automobile. More than an ancient joke, "Pahk the cah in Hahvad Yahd" was sound advice for anyone foolish enough to drive to Fenway Park.

And so the Sox spent the final decade of the 20th century trying with renewed vigor to kill this ancient creature. There was the proposed "Megaplex," a sports-and-convention center on Northern Avenue. There were various plans to build a new park next to Fenway (and a new Pats stadium next to that) with parking for both suspended above the Massachusetts Turnpike. In 1995, two Cambridge architects proposed putting not the parking garage but the new ballpark itself above the Mass Pike, evidently on the grounds that if you couldn't drive *to* a Red Sox game, you could at least drive *under* one.

The team had by then decided that renovating Fenway was inadequate. There would be no Band-Aids on Updike's bandbox of a ballpark. The team announced its intention in 1995 to have a new home by that futuristic year of 2001. Owner John Harrington told a state commission that Fenway would remain structurally sound only until 2005 or so, but was already "economically obsolete," rendering the team unable to compete with his luxury-boxed brethren in the Bronx and elsewhere.

And so a new stadium site was being pushed in South Boston, to be developed by a Boston real-estate magnate. That project died, like all those before it, in a thicket of politics, red tape and residential opposition, and the thwarted developer would go on to buy the Los Angeles Dodgers. Mr. Frank McCourt proceeded to plunge that franchise into bankruptcy, suggesting that Fenway had dodged a bullet, a silver bullet, as the ballpark was by now a full-blown horror-movie monster—apparently immortal, but almost certain to die in the final reel.

One thing was certain: The new Fenway Park—whatever it was, wherever it was—would not be called Fenway Park, but something more remunerative. "If AT&T or New England Telephone want to pay $50 million and name the park after them," a Sox executive told the *Globe* in 1996, "tell 'em to come talk."

The 1999 All-Star Game, then, seemed a farewell to Fenway. The latest $300 million park being proposed on 14 acres adjacent to the ballpark—let's call it New England Telephone Stadium, for maximum grotesquerie—was to have the Green Monster transplanted into it and the brickwork facade transplanted onto it, creating a Frankenstein's monster of old and new.

The stake was on the heart, and the mallet was being raised when, in December of 2001, John Henry and Tom Werner bought the Red Sox and set about straightening the Leaning Tower of Pisa. They at once renovated the park and the team, neither of which had seen a world championship since the fall of 1918, when Harry Frazee celebrated by making that first fumbling attempt to flee Fenway.

You know the rest of the story: How the Sox, in 2004, with a ritual shedding of blood, finally won the World Series again in a revamped—a revampired?—Fenway Park. The victory came as a great relief to countless fans, among them Stephen King, the most renowned horror novelist since Bram Stoker, to whom he is tied not just through genre but through Fenway, a monster every bit as unkillable as any other conjured by man.

AUTHOR UPDIKE (TOP) EXALTED
the old ballpark, Tiger Stadium failed to outlast it, and author King, on many occasions, has reveled in it.

A BELOVED AND IRREGULAR PLACE

Destined from the beginning to be architecturally quirky, Fenway Park, for all its cosmetic changes, remains an unspoiled haven for baseball

BY TOM VERDUCCI

WHEN, IN 1911, BOSTON RED SOX owner Gen. Charles Taylor asked Osborne Engineering and architect James McLaughlin to build him a ballpark, he ordered it to fit inside an irregular, angular chunk of property he purchased in the Fenway district, the former mudflats known as the Fens. It was the equivalent of commissioning a painting and handing the master the size and shape of canvas to fill. Taylor gave McLaughlin one further piece of instruction: The third base line must point virtually due north so that the orientation toward the sun matched that of the Huntington Avenue Grounds, the home the Red Sox were leaving. This order left McLaughlin with little more than 300 feet between home plate and the hard stop represented by Lansdowne Street, which formed the northern boundary of the property; but it also mandated a veritable trolley ride of 550 feet to the northeast corner where centerfield would end.

One hundred years later, what bound Fenway Park is what unbinds us. When we sit in Fenway's precious few seats, most especially the wood-slat ones behind home plate that have been there for more than 70 years, we are transported to places of history and of the heart unreachable anywhere else. The beauty of Fenway is its very unconformity, what John Updike nimbly called "a compromise between man's Euclidean determinations and nature's beguiling irregularities." Its angles, quirks, doorways, ladders, slats, poles and pillars bear no hint of contrivance. When the American Institute of Architects put Fenway on its list of the 150 buildings that defined the "Shape of America," Gary Wolf of AIA noted, "The odd thing about Fenway is that probably of the top 150 buildings that we're dealing with on the list, this one exhibits the least sense of intentional design by one hand."

One day before a game late last season, Red Sox second baseman Dustin Pedroia sat in the shoebox of a home dugout—where players must still navigate around pillars—and said in wonderment, "A hundred years. This place is a hundred years old? Imagine that." It was easy to imagine Tris Speaker or Ted Williams or Carlton Fisk or Roger Clemens taking in the same view from the same dugout. The ballpark has made for a rare unbroken line that connects those who have worn the Red Sox uniform, as well as those who have rooted for them.

FENWAY HAS TAKEN ON A FEELING OF CIVic grounds rather than sacred ones. It is more town hall than cathedral. When Taylor chose the spot for the ballpark, Kenmore Square was just beginning to grow. But it was Fenway that became the bigger public square. As people gather inside the park, sitting in the seats sat in by their fathers, grandfathers and great-grandfathers, they can gaze upon what have become the physical shorthand notes of civic pride: the Yaz Door, Pesky Pole, Fisk Pole, DiMaggio Flag Pole, the Triangle, Canvas Alley, the hand-operated scoreboard, the Yawkey Morse Code, Williamsburg, the Williams Red Seat and, looming above all in size and theatrical value, the Wall.

The Wall was an oddity when the park opened on April 20, 1912: 25 feet high, made of wood and built atop a 10-foot embankment. But The Wall had an important purpose, preventing fans from seeing games for free, keeping them from climbing in without tickets or from observing the game from Lansdowne rooftops without having to pay.

It was after the 1933 season, during a massive reconstruction of Fenway ordered by new team owner Thomas Yawkey, that the Wall was rebuilt into its current form: 240 feet long and 37 feet, two inches high. Two years later a 23½-foot-high swath of netting was added to catch home run balls. Another major change came in 1947, when Yawkey removed huge advertisements from the Wall and painted it what is now an iconic green. Known as Fenway Green, the color is patented and not commercially available (though, to be fair, Benjamin Moore's "fence green" is nearly identical); the new paint job caused the Wall to become known as the Green Monster.

Finally, seats were added atop the Green Monster in 2003, as if a jury box on high. These 269 Monster Seats provide the most stunning view available in baseball without the use of a blimp; best of all, having been designed by the architect Janet Marie Smith, they seem more an integration with than an addition to the ballpark. The restoration of "America's Most Beloved Ballpark" was so successful that it fools you into thinking the place always was mythic and adored. Not so.

In the visiting manager's office, for instance, hangs a picture of Opening Day 1963 at Fenway, with rows of empty seats. (Attendance was 26,161.) When Ted Williams homered in his last at bat, a 1960 event made momentous by John

A LADIES DAY GAME IN 1946 LURED a fashionable crowd, lined up along Jersey Street for tickets to see the Red Sox take on the Detroit Tigers.
Photograph by BOSTON PUBLIC LIBRARY

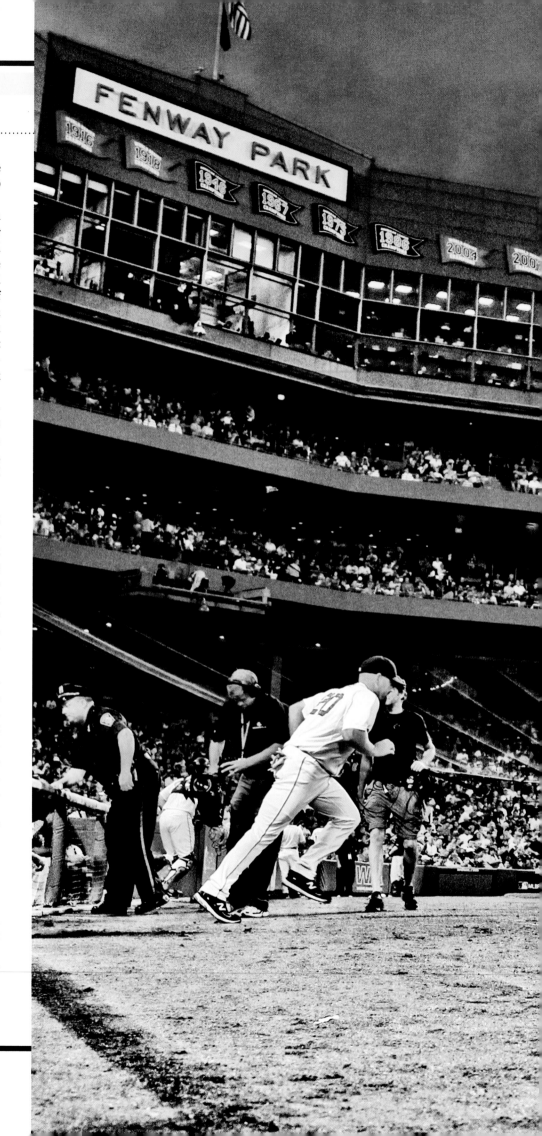

Updike's *New Yorker* essay "Hub Fans Bid Kid Adieu," Updike was one of only 10,454 fans on hand—the previous day 5,840 had shown up.

The most unhappy news came in an announcement on May 15, 1999, by John Harrington, who ran the Red Sox for the Yawkey Trust that owned the team, that Fenway would be replaced in 2003 by a "modern Fenway," a ballpark to be built behind Fenway's home plate that looked like Fenway and would have the same dimensions as Fenway. But not the soul of Fenway. A facsimile. A Faux Fenway. The proposed destruction of the old park, a portion of which would be "preserved" akin to a museum relic, had its supporters. *Boston Globe* columnist Bob Ryan, witnessing a building boom around baseball as Fenway fell into disrepair, said the Red Sox needed a new ballpark "unequivocally. There really is nothing to debate."

Grassroots opposition and a downturn in economic conditions forestalled Harrington's plans, and by the time Henry's group bought the team in 2001, not one brick had been torn down. Three years later, with restorations so well received, Henry's group announced that Fenway—the real thing—would be the Red Sox' home "for generations."

FENWAY IS COMFORT FOOD FOR THE baseball soul. There is nothing majestic, colossal or pretentious about it. The story goes that when a taxi dropped off Clemens for the first time at Fenway, he gazed upon the park's humble, low profile and told the driver he must be mistaken, that this must be a warehouse, not a major league ballpark. Fenway is history made accessible. It is less the building itself and more this shared experience—this "communal comfort" preserved— that allows Fenway to transport us.

One of Fenway's many charms, rising from the manual scoreboard up the Green Monster, is a ladder that is in play, as if left by forgetful janitors. It was placed there in 1936 when Yawkey hung that net above the Wall. Each day after batting practice an attendant would climb the ladder and fish baseballs out of the net. Dick Stuart, a lumbering Red Sox first baseman in the mid-1960s, once clanked a drive off the ladder, which sent the ball flying in a direction unexpected by outfielders, allowing for an only-in-Fenway home run. The Monster Seats have made the ladder moot, what with the net gone and home run balls becoming souvenirs for the lucky souls perched there.

Still, the ladder remains. It has become, in the arcana of Fenway, the Ladder to Nowhere. It is said to have its own ground rule: Should a fly ball lodge in the ladder, the batter is awarded a triple—the only ground-rule triple in baseball. It appears, however, to be an apocryphal notion. That the rule may be a myth, or that the ladder goes nowhere, is unimportant. What matters is that the ladder winks at us, and we are in on this little totemic witticism of living history. The ladder is a proxy for all of Fenway. Knowing that it has been there is important, though not quite as important as knowing that it will be there.

IN ITS THIRD SEASON, FENWAY PARK,
tightly constructed between Lansdowne Street (left) and
Jersey Street (right), played host to the 1914 World Series;
but it was the Boston Braves, not the Red Sox, who were
the home team, taking on the Philadelphia Athletics.

Digital composite by PANOPTICON/BOSTON PUBLIC LIBRARY PRINT DEPARTMENT

THE POWER OF

The author, in 1965, posited that Fenway's leftfield wall, for all its charm, had induced a troubling effect on the Red Sox

BY JACK MANN

Excerpted from **SPORTS ILLUSTRATED** 6.28.65

AS A TARGET, THE GREEN Monster has long been a huge temptation for righthanded hitters—like Jose Canseco in '95.
Photograph by CHUCK SOLOMON

THE WALL

379
115.5

PAPER
YES

et Bar

HE WINDOW HIGH OVER THE DOOR IN THE BACK of the Pennant Grille, at the corner of Lansdowne Street and Brookline Avenue in Boston, is painted opaque. The reason for the obscurity is obscure, but it may have saved any number of Boston Red Sox fans from acute depression. Through a clear window a drinking man in the Pennant Grille can see the Fenway Park wall, the principal reason why no pennant has fluttered over the Grille for 19 years, and only one in the 46 seasons since World War I. That 37-foot-high leftfield fence, topped by its 23-foot-high basket of baseball-catching chicken wire, could make a fan on the outside feel—like a pitcher on the inside—a prisoner of Fenway Park.

The Fenway wall is the most famous of the structural idiosyncrasies so common in the major league ballparks that were built half a century ago, and now that the Polo Grounds and Ebbets Field are gone it is one of the few remaining in this era of new, large and symmetrical stadiums. It starts near the leftfield foul line, only 315 feet from home plate, and juts at a right angle 275 feet across the outfield until it meets the centerfield bleachers. It is the most inviting target for a righthanded hitter in the major leagues; fly balls become base hits and would-be home runs that don't quite make it to the chicken wire ricochet off the wall below for doubles.

Hitters love it and pitchers hate it, and it drives managers crazy; both hitters and pitchers tend to alter their natural style of play to take account of the wall, and this too often adversely affects their play when they are away from Fenway. Because abrupt adjustment from the incongruities of Fenway to the symmetry of other parks is almost impossible, Red Sox teams over the years have accepted consistent inconsistency (since World War II a .607 winning percentage at home compared to .446 on the road) as their manifest destiny. And Bostonians have faithfully embraced the team as a poor thing but their own. Nobody gets hurt except 62-year-old owner Thomas A. Yawkey. After more than half a lifetime of loving the game and his players not at all wisely and much too well, he sits in

VERN STEPHENS AND
Walt Dropo were two of
the righthanded sluggers
brought to Fenway to take
aim at the Wall.
Photograph by BETTMANN/CORBIS

his gilded cage atop the Fenway roof and hopes. He listens for promises ("threats," he calls them) of the extravagant new Boston stadium that might soon be authorized by the Commonwealth of Massachusetts, liberating him to assemble the kind of team and play the kind of baseball he has wanted since he became the Sox' Daddy Warbucks in 1933.

"Hit and run," Yawkey says. "Steal a base. That's the way I like to play the game. I say the hell with the fence and play as if you were in Comiskey Park."

But, Yawkey's advisers told him, he couldn't have that kind of team because the fence was there. Got to have righthand hitters, pull hitters, hit the wall.

They hit the wall in 1946—Rudy York, Bobby Doerr, Mike Higgins, Dom DiMaggio—and proved the point. The Red Sox were 61–16 in Fenway, an overwhelming .792 percentage, and they won the pennant. They lost the World Series by dropping three of four games to the Cardinals in St. Louis, of course, but the formula had been established.

In 1948 they played .714 ball at home (the pace of the fabled 1927 Yankees) but lost the pennant to Cleveland in a one-game playoff. By 1949 the Red Sox had obtained Vern Stephens, the American League's premier righthanded pull hitter of the time. He tapped the wall for 159 RBIs, the Sox hit .282 as a team and won 61 games at home again. But this time they were seven games under .500 on the road and the Yankees beat them out on the last day of the season.

The thunder increased in 1950 and so did the frustration. Now the Red Sox had Walt Dropo, another very strong right-handed pull hitter, at first base. He and Stephens batted in 144 runs each and the team batting average was .302. Boston finished third. Fourteen years and seven managers have gone by, and only three times since have they finished as high.

"We've done very well at home," Yawkey says. "If we'd been able to play .500 ball on the road we'd have been a lot higher. But dammit, that wall hurts: It has an effect on the organization from top to bottom. We have to go after players who have that Fenway stroke, but then they get in the habit of pulling the ball and they try it on the road and it's no good. Hitters' habits are hard to break."

Other little flaws in the "Fenway stroke" theory became screechingly obvious. First of all, very few of the big, strong righthanded pull hitters are either deft fielders or swift runners. Secondly, even fewer feel that they have to be. Ted Williams's total of 521 home runs, hitting lefthanded toward Fenway's elongated rightfield for half his career, has always seemed one of baseball's most remarkable records, but there is another that stands out. For a lefthanded pitcher to win at all in Fenway is notable, but in 1949 Mel Parnell won 25 games and had a 2.78 earned-run average.

"I don't see how a lefthander could do that," says Bill Monbouquette, Boston's most successful righthanded pitcher of recent years. "You have to keep every pitch down, and against the righthanders you can only use the outside part of the plate."

"Think about the wall?" says Dave Morehead, the bright rookie righthander, when asked about its influence. "You don't think about anything else." When Sal Maglie was the Red Sox' pitching coach he tried to get across one message. A different ballpark, he said, doesn't make you a different pitcher. You have to pitch your way and make the batter hit your pitch. But Sal's words fell on deaf ears: It is incalculable how many sore arms have resulted from pitchers' unnatural attempts to avoid the Fenway stroke.

Or how many hitters the wall has led astray. Billy Herman, who became the manager this year, would like to play the kind of baseball Yawkey would like to play. "I like to hit and run and I like to steal a base," Herman says. "But I can't steal that much, because we don't have that kind of speed, and we can't hit and run because we don't have the hitters who can meet the ball." Besides, he explains, "You've got to play that wall here because you know the other teams will."

Boston's Ed Bressoud is just an adequate shortstop, but he is a practitioner of the Fenway stroke and hits home runs, or what pass for home runs in Fenway. Herman writes Bressoud name into the lineup instead of the fine-fielding, 21-year-old shortstop Rico Petrocelli, who doesn't hit home runs. With his glove Petrocelli is reminiscent of another kid shortstop the Red Sox might have taken a look at in the fall of 1939. He was on their Louisville farm, the Red Sox weren't going to catch the Yankees anyway and their shortstop, Joe Cronin, was getting old. But Cronin was the manager too. So Yawkey took $40,000 and four faceless players for the kid. His name was Harold Reese.

Pee Wee Reese, who would go on to play on seven pennant-winning teams for the Brooklyn Dodgers, was the "different kind of player" Yawkey talked about for 10 years before he did something about it in 1960. He named Dick O'Connell, a businessman, as executive vice president, and O'Connell's first official act was to shake up the scouting network, which needed it. When Yawkey liked a player—and Yawkey falls in love with players—he wanted to keep him on the payroll, so the scouting system became a sort of pension pool. "Give him a territory," the word was. One superannuated pitcher received three paychecks before he found out he was a scout. When a particular territory was not heard from for any length of time, it was simply assumed that no righthanded pull hitters had been turned up and there was nothing to report.

That has changed. It is emphasized around Fenway these days that the 10 batting championships the Red Sox have won over the past 24 seasons have all been by lefthanded batters: Ted Williams, Billy Goodman, Pete Runnels and Carl Yastrzemski.

Yawkey has seen black ink only six times in his first 32 years in Boston, and it is no disillusion to him that the blind loyalty of New England fans has been less visible at the turnstiles since 1960. "The only way to do better," he says, "is to win. They shake your hand and wish you well at Rotary meetings, but they don't show up. All they care about—I don't give a damn what anybody says—is the won-lost record."

One way to win is to have the best players. The Red Sox did in 1946, but coincidentally that was the year Jackie Robinson—who had been tried in Fenway Park and found wanting—played his first year in organized (white) baseball. In the parade of Larry Dobys and Roy Campanellas and Elston Howards that followed, the Red Sox brought up the rear. Pumpsie Green became the Red Sox' first Negro big leaguer in 1959. It is easy now for Bostonian critics, seeking a policy man behind such a self-defeating pattern, to point fingers at Mike Higgins, an unreconstructed Texan with classically Confederate views, but it is too easy. Higgins did not become field manager until 1955 and did not take a desk in the front office until late 1962. "They blame me," Yawkey says, "and I'm not even a Southerner. I'm from Detroit."

HE MANAGERS HAVE TRIED over the years since Joe McCarthy's two near pennants in the late 1940s to lift the club, but they have not been much help. Billy Herman is a compromise between the laissez-faire of Mike ("they're grown men") Higgins and the abortive attempts of Lou Boudreau, Billy Jurges and Johnny Pesky to "build a fire" under a complacent team. Pesky, despite a run-in with Yastrzemski that smoldered on in mutual hatred, might have been something like the manager the Red Sox needed, except for two things: 1) he tried to do too much too soon to change attitudes too long established and, 2) he was too sensitive to the barbs of the Boston press.

The Boston press takes some getting used to. In a time when it is a rarity to see an old-fashioned competitive press in a smaller city, editions of Boston's metropolitan papers pop out at all odd hours of the day and night, and the city is ringed by lively suburban dailies that want to—and do—get in the act. With 10 papers double-and triple-teaming the Red Sox' home games, Fenway's is often the only press box more populous than those in New York.

"You have to understand something else," says a Bostonian. "All the writers in Boston are ball fans. Sure, they're sarcastic and cynical about the club, and they're always ripping somebody. But there's a reason for that. When those guys go to spring training, they see a new shortstop who looks pretty good, and they get carried away because they want to believe he's that good. Then in May the kid is hitting .191 and they're sore as hell. They feel deceived. It's like they fell in love with some broad and she took off with

another guy. They're sore all the time because they're fans."

Comes now the crowning irony. The same Boston press is honing its hatchets for the new stadium and arena plan to be presented by Governor John Volpe's three-man commission at the end of June. It is as true as it was when Tom Yawkey first surveyed his new holdings in 1933 that there is not room to play baseball between Lansdowne and Jersey Streets, and nothing would help the Sox as much as a new, spacious playground. But if the Boston press is composed of fans it is also composed of taxpayers. Even if they live in Quincy or Worcester or Wellesley, they are taxpayers to the Commonwealth of Massachusetts, which is uncommonly short of wealth these days.

The total expense, says Monsignor George Kerr, a member of the stadium commission, would approximate $87 million, because the new Boston stadium would outdome Houston. Boston's would have a roof, of course, but the roof would be retractable. "Railroad property is available at the end of the new turnpike," Msgr. Kerr says, "in the South Station area. A parking garage is needed anyway, because the area is very adjacent to the center of Boston. An arena is necessary because Boston Garden is obsolete because of parking. So is Fenway Park, for the same reason. We have talked to bonding companies and they approve the plan. It would be one of the few stadiums in the country built with private capital. Of course, the property would revert to the state after 40 years."

And nothing can be done without the Red Sox. But Yawkey is wary from experience of political negotiations in Boston. He has tried "about 20 times" for clearance to close Lansdowne Street and move the wall back. He could have bought up the complex of liquor distributorships across the street, where the real home runs land, and the street would no longer be needed. "But this is the only big league city that is also a state capital," Yawkey points out. "You have to deal on two political levels. You get agreement from the state and you find you've lost the city."

Rapport between the city and state on any $87 million new playground seemed highly unlikely as the day neared for the presentation of the plan. At about that time, as Mayor John Collins of Boston was pointing out, the Commonwealth would owe the city about $13,650,000 in welfare funds. The legislators, he scolded, would have to keep other costs down.

And the Fenway wall would stay up, and the Red Sox hitters and pitchers would continue to live in its shadow. They needn't worry. They don't have to win, and the pay is good.

POSTSCRIPT *The grand plan for a new domed stadium, of course, never came to pass; a paucity of support for public financing doomed the idea. The Fenway Wall stood firm, known with growing affection to all as the Green Monster, its place in the iconography of Fenway Park, and baseball, ever more elevated. And in time, even the Fenway Wall could not stand between the Red Sox and another championship.*

CARL YASTRZEMSKI, WHO made a sensational catch at the Wall on a Curt Flood drive in the '67 World Series, conquered the Green Monster effect as a lefty batter.
Photograph by BETTMANN/CORBIS

< **IN 1912, THE WALL WAS** one giant billboard; for that year's World Series (here Game 2), temporary stands were built at the base of the Wall for additional seating.
Photograph by LESLIE JONES

∧ **BY THE TIME TRIS** Speaker, the Sox centerfielder, ran the bases in 1915, the 10-foot incline beneath the wall was known as Duffy's Cliff, for leftfielder Duffy Lewis who'd mastered how to play it.
Photograph by BETTMANN/CORBIS

THERE IS NO BETTER STAGE SET IN baseball for a dramatic play (this one by Jason Bay) than Fenway's famous Wall.
Photograph by DAMIAN STROHMEYER

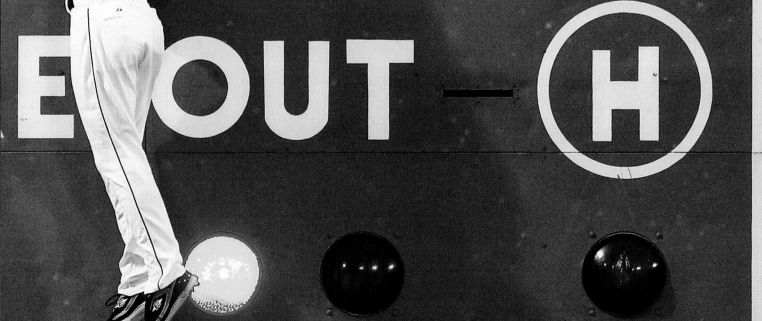

< **SCOREBOARD OPERATOR**
James Stokes eyed a
Boston–New York game in
'87, then posted the final:
Sox 4, Yanks 2.

Photograph by WALTER IOOSS JR.

∧ **ALONGSIDE THE NAMES**
and numbers to be hand-
hung on the scoreboard
are the scribblings
of past visitors.

Photographs by HEINZ KLUETMEIER

THE WALL WAS THE backdrop for the career of Ted Williams, who owned leftfield for 18 seasons.
Photograph by WILLIAM C. GREENE

OVER THE YEARS, ANY number of celebrities— such as John McEnroe (above) and Jimmy Buffett—have had the chance to pop their famous faces out of the small window between the ball and strike lights. But at game time, it's for employees only.

Photographs by BETHANY VERSOY, MAILBOAT RECORDS *and* BETTMANN/CORBIS

∧ **DURING THE '80S, WHEN**
Jim Rice refined his skill at
working a ball off the Wall,
the Monster was ad-free,
beautifully clean and green.
Photograph by JOHN D. HANLON

< **WHEN BOSTON PLAYED**
the Yankees in '42, the
Wall was a monument to
whiskey and razor blades.
In '47, all ads came down,
green paint went up, and
"the Wall" became "the
Green Monster."
Photograph by MARGARET MAYALL

33 MIN

38 BOST

AT BAT

^ **A MEMBER OF BOSTON'S**
Finest patrolled the Wall after
the Red Sox shut out the Cardinals
in Game 2 of the '67 Series.
Photograph by NEIL LEIFER

> **THE WALL AFFORDED**
effective home field advantage
when Carlos Lee of Chicago got
snagged in 2003.
Photograph by STANLEY HU

< **DURING A PITCHING**
break in an '05 game, Manny
Ramirez disappeared then
reemerged from the scoreboard.
It was speculated that Manny
sought to answer nature's call.
Photograph by CHARLES KRUPA

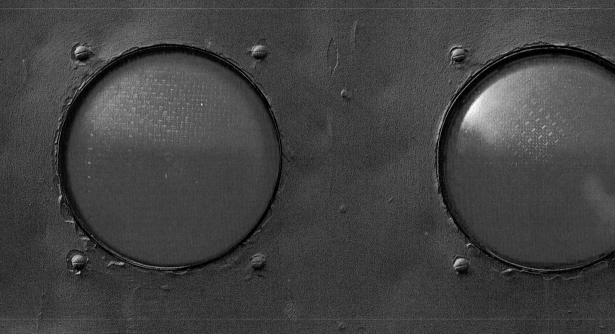

STRIK

PITCHER PEDRO MARTINEZ IN '99
got comfortable with his preferred part
of the scoreboard. By season's end, he led
the AL in strikeouts with 313.
Photograph by V.J. LOVERO

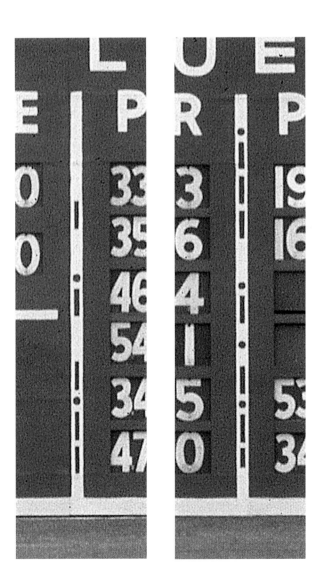

< **THE WALL BECAME A** temporary shrine to Ted Williams in 2002, two weeks after his death.
Photograph by VICTORIA AROCHO

∨ **THE VERTICAL SERIES** of dots and dashes on the scoreboard, added in 1947, represent the initials in Morse code of Thomas Austin Yawkey (TAY, on the left) and Jean Remington. Yawkey (JRY)—a favorite piece of Fenway arcana.
Photographs by WALTER IOOSS JR.

< **FOR 67 YEARS, THE NET**
behind the Wall, 23 feet
high, caught most of the
home runs that passed over.
Photograph by AL BELLO

∧ **WHEN THE SEATS WERE**
built on top of the Monster
in '03, the net was gone and
fans got a shot at a catch.
Photograph by CHARLES KRUPA

⌐ **THE SEATS ATOP THE GREEN**
Monster, first available for the
2003 season, quickly became
the most desired of all.
Photograph by DAN NERNEY

∧ **MO VAUGHN, HIS SMALL**
friend and the big Green
Monster appeared on the
cover of SI in 1995.
Photograph by WALTER IOOSS JR.

< **A FAN FAVORITE AT**
Fenway, Dustin Pedroia posed
in front of the Wall with some
of his younger admirers.
Photograph by HEINZ KLUETMEIER

> **THE GREEN MONSTER, ITS**
appellation now 64 years old,
is more than a nickname; it's
a living civic monument.
Photograph by SHAUN BEST

GREEN
MONSTER

3

GREEN
MONSTER

4

5

6

VOLVO

COVIDIEN

FENWAY PARK 99th ANNIVERSARY

BOSTON RED SOX
TOGETHER SINCE 1953
THE JIMMY FUND

ENWAY PARK
1 2 3 4 5 6 7 8 9 10 | R H E
2 | 2 3
| 0

ALL STRIKE OUT (H) (E)

AMERICAN LEAGUE				
P	IN R	P	IN R	
31 CLE	N	62 MIN	N	
45 TEX		44 KC		
31 DET		47 NYY	N	
39 CWS		38 SEA		
36 LAA	N	40 TB	N	
18 OAK		46 BAL		

NATIONAL LEAGUE				
P	IN R	P	IN R	
40 COL		41 ARI	N	38 SD	N
18 MIL		22 LAD		55 SF	
27 CHC		34 PHI		41 WSH	N
47 CIN		20 HOU		NYM	
FLA	7 0	22 STL		
TL	7 0	50 PIT		

F.W. WEBB

Since WEBB 1866

THE PRESENT-DAY MONSTER HAS
returned to the age of advertising,
albeit less colorful—or, to be
precise, more green.
Photograph by DAMIAN STROHMEYER

1912 TO 2011

A Timeline

100 YEARS

OF FENWAY

1912 TO 1919

Fenway Park opens ~ Red Sox win four world championships in eight seasons ~ 50,000 pack the park to see three elephants ~ Babe Ruth is sold to the Yankees

Donnelly Bill Poster

RUETER & COMPANY ALE AND PORTER BOSTON BREWERS

Sterling Ale

April 20, 1912
The first two scheduled Red Sox games at the new Fenway Park are rained out. Third try is a charm: sunshine, Sox win.
Photograph by NATIONAL BASEBALL HALL OF FAME

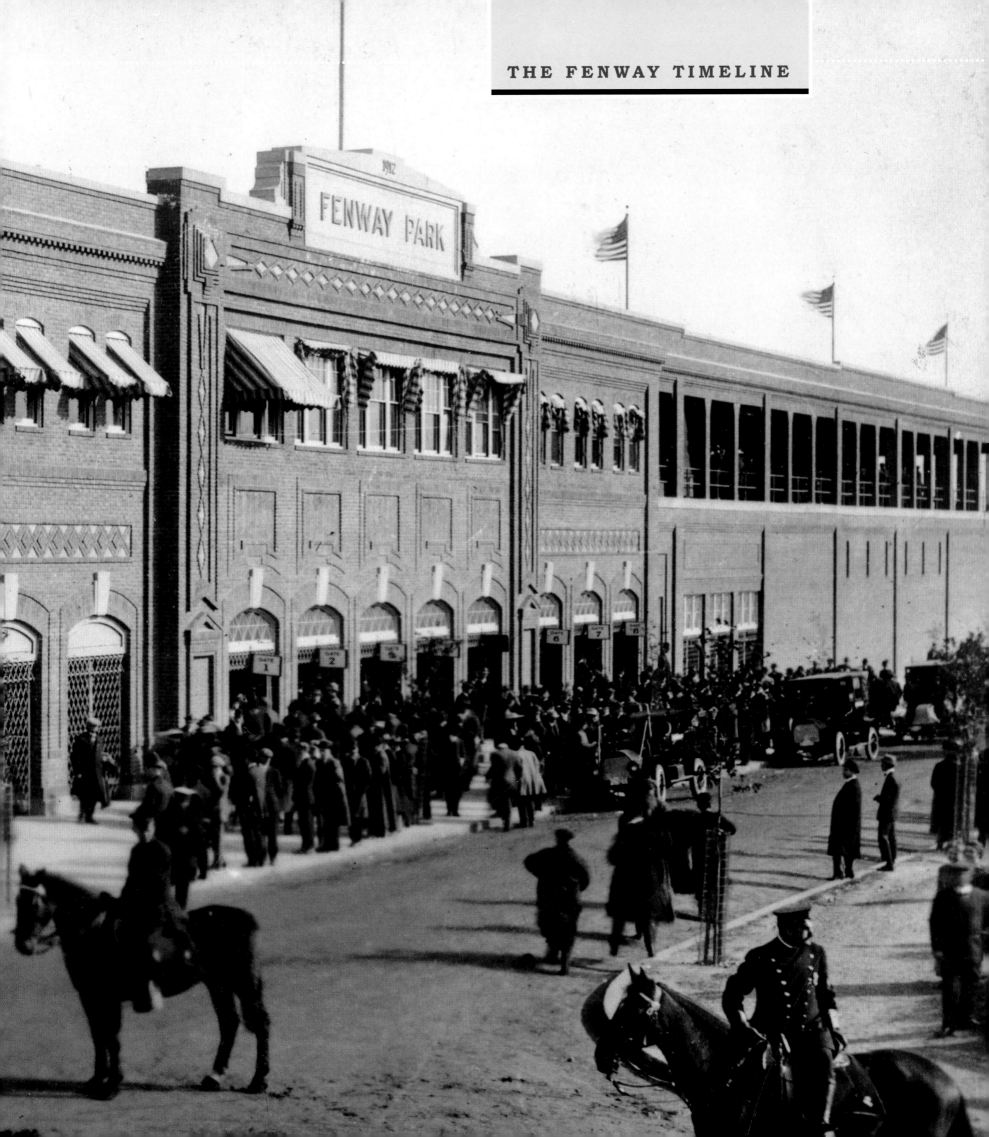

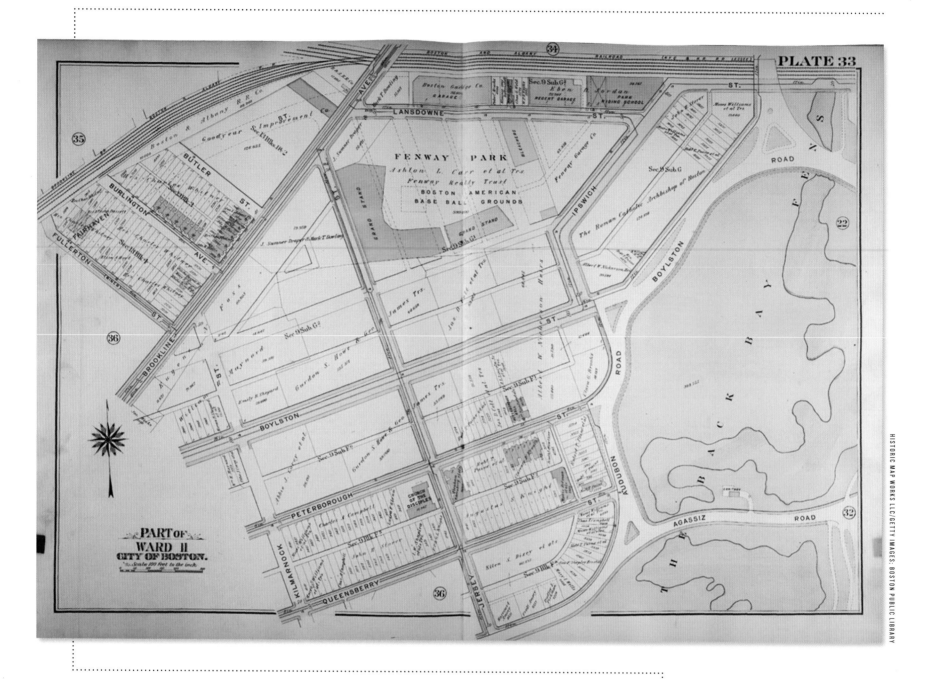

PLATE 33

FENWAY PARK
Ashton L. Carr et al Trs
Fenway Realty Trust
BOSTON AMERICAN
BASE BALL GROUNDS

PART OF
WARD 11
CITY OF BOSTON.
Scale 100 feet to the inch

1912

>>>>>>

... "TITANIC" SINKS AFTER
STRIKING ICEBERG... JIM
THORPE WINS DECATHLON AND
PENTATHLON AT STOCKHOLM
OLYMPICS... GIRL SCOUTS OF THE
USA IS FOUNDED...

< APRIL 20

Fenway Park is on the map. On Opening
Day at the new stadium, Charles Logue, the
contractor who supervised construction,
stands by his work. The Red Sox then beat
the New York Highlanders 7–6

APRIL 26 >

Red Sox first baseman Hugh
Bradley hits the first Fenway home
run, over the leftfield wall. It will be
Bradley's only homer of the season

BRADLEY-BOSTON-AMER.

OCTOBER 16 >

The Royal Rooters fan club, with Red Sox mascot Jerry McCarthy, celebrates a World Series title, won by beating the New York Giants and Christy Mathewson. Series bleacher seats at Fenway: 50 cents

< **SEPTEMBER 6**

Sox ace Smokey Joe Wood outduels Washington Senators ace Walter Johnson 1-0. It is Wood's 14th consecutive win

CHAMPIONS 1912
RED SOX
WORLD'S SERIES
Fenway Park Boston
Souvenir Biography and Score Book
Price, 10 Cents

1913

> > > > > >

...FRANCIS OUIMET WINS U.S. OPEN AT THE COUNTRY CLUB IN BROOKLINE...U.S. FEDERAL RESERVE SYSTEM IS ESTABLISHED ...FIRST MODERN CROSSWORD PUZZLE IS PUBLISHED IN THE "NEW YORK WORLD"...

AUG 28

For the third time this season, Sox lefty Ray Collins faces Walter Johnson; for the third time, the final is 1-0, as Collins wins two of them, including this one, in 11 innings

WORLD SERIES FOR RENT

The Red Sox aren't the only Boston baseball team to win a championship at Fenway

T HEY ARE REMEMBERED as the "Miracle Braves," and the name is no exaggeration. Boston's other ball club—under the monikers Beaneaters then Doves then Rustlers then Braves—had suffered a miserable run in the National League through the first 13 seasons of the century. Things were no better on the Fourth of July 1914; the Braves were 26–40 and 15 games out of first place, playing before small home crowds at the South End Grounds. The season looked dead.

But a month later, the streaking Braves were just 7½ games out of first. On Aug. 3, Red Sox president Joe Lannin sent a telegram to Braves owner James Gaffney offering to rent him the larger Fenway Park for the rest of the season free of charge. "I want to see Mr. Gaffney reap the benefits of good luck," Lannin said. (A sporting miracle in its own right.)

On Sept. 8, the Braves beat New York Giants 8–3 to move into first and would win the NL by an unlikely 10½ games. The Braves would then sweep Connie Mack's heavily favored Philadelphia Athletics in October. The team moved to its new Braves Field the following summer. In 1953, they would depart for Milwaukee, but they left behind an indelible championship mark on Fenway.

LEFTFIELDER JOE CONNOLLY

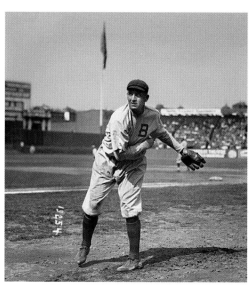

PITCHER BILL JAMES

SHORTSTOP RABBIT MARANVILLE

PITCHER DICK RUDOLPH

1914

〉〉〉〉〉〉

...ASSASSINATION OF AUSTRIAN ARCHDUKE FERDINAND SPARKS WORLD WAR I...PANAMA CANAL OPENS...RED AND GREEN TRAFFIC LIGHTS FIRST USED, IN CLEVELAND...

〈 **JUNE 6**

Over 50,000 people jam Fenway to see Mollie, Tony and Waddy—a trio of elephants bought for the Franklin Park Zoo with $6,700 raised by schoolchildren

JULY 11 〉

A 19-year-old rookie pitcher, George Ruth, makes his Red Sox debut and gets the win, beating the Cleveland Naps 4–3. The Babe, as his teammates call him, goes 0 for 2 at the plate

^
AUGUST 17

Former President Theodore Roosevelt attends Progressive Party Field Day at Fenway, a track and field competition

1915

›››››

... FIRE KILLS 21 GIRLS AT ST.
JOHN'S SCHOOL IN PEABODY ...
FEDERAL LEAGUE BASEBALL PLAYS
SECOND AND FINAL SEASON ...
D.W. GRIFFITH FILM "BIRTH OF A
NATION" PREMIERES ...

JULY 26

The defending world
champion Boston Braves
play their final home game
at Fenway, beating the
Cubs 1-0, then go on a
19-game road trip before
moving into their new
Boston home, Braves Field

SEPTEMBER 18

From the original, ornate
rooftop press box at Fenway,
scribes watch the Red Sox beat
the Detroit Tigers 1-0

OCTOBER 11 ›

Boston star Tris Speaker and
Phillies outfielder Gavvy Cravath pose
before World Series Game 3 (played at
Braves Field due to larger capacity). Sox
will win the Series four games to one

‹ SEPTEMBER 27

The Sox win their 99th game en route to a
101-50 season, led by "The Golden Outfield" of Tris
Speaker, Duffy Lewis and Harry Hooper. Hooper
(using this glove, left) will become the only man to
play on four Red Sox championship teams

1916

>>>>>>

*...ALBERT EINSTEIN PUBLISHES
THEORY OF GENERAL RELATIVITY
...JEANNETTE RANKIN OF
MONTANA IS FIRST WOMAN
ELECTED TO U.S. CONGRESS...
CHICK EVANS IS FIRST GOLFER TO
WIN U.S. AMATEUR AND U.S. OPEN
IN SAME YEAR...*

^ JUNE 20

Boston's Everett Scott (second from
left above) starts at shortstop, beginning a
streak of 1,307 consecutive games played,
a major league record that would last until
broken by Lou Gehrig. The Sox 1916 infield
(from left): Larry Gardner (3B), Scott, Jack
Barry (2B) and Dick Hoblitzell (1B)

‹ JUNE 21

Boston righthander
George (Rube) Foster
throws the first no-
hitter by a Red Sox
pitcher in Fenway,
beating the Yankees 2-0

Boston American League Base Ball Club
Fenway Park
Admit *M. T. McGreevy*
During Season of 1916
This Pass Book is NOT TRANSFERABLE. It will be forfeited and taken
up by Gate Keeper if presented by any other than person named above, and
holder's name will be stricken from Pass List and further courtesies will not be
extended. Coupons must be detached only by Gate Keeper.
Sign your name on back inside Cover.
No. 013   *Jeff S_____*
                                              President

^ OCTOBER 3

The Red Sox take the AL pennant, pleasing
credentialed fan Michael T. McGreevy, saloon owner
and leader of the Royal Roooters. Boston will beat
Brooklyn in the World Series four games to one.

Excerpted from **BABE: THE LEGEND COMES TO LIFE**

BY ROBERT W. CREAMER

A MISPLACED MASTERPIECE

In 1916 Red Sox pitcher Babe Ruth was the best lefty in baseball, with a 1.75 ERA and 23 wins, and beloved at Fenway. Oddly, his greatest home victory happened two miles away

BOSTON'S ROYAL ROOTERS were much in evidence before Game 2 on the afternoon of Oct. 9, 1916, sitting in a group, complete with red-coated band, near the Red Sox dugout. [The Sox home dugout was in fact the dugout of the Boston Braves; it is a peculiar twist in the history of Fenway Park that the Red Sox decided to play their home games in the 1915 and '16 World Series at Braves Field, with some 5,000 more seats than Fenway, to pack in a larger crowd. But the most devout Sox fans, the Royal Rooters, made the place feel like their Fenway home, where the Sox had dominated all year, going 49–28.]

Over and over the band played and the Rooters sang a tune called *Tessie*, which for some inane reason had become their Fenway fight song. "Tessie," they sang, "you make me feel so bahadly. Why don't you turn around? Tessie, you know I love you sadly, babe. My heart weighs about a pound." Tessie might have been popular with the Royal Rooters, but followers of rival teams found her an agonizing bore. "That measly, monotonous melody," one newspaperman called it, but the Rooters sang it gleefully, soulfully and repeatedly.

When Babe Ruth took the mound to start what was to become one of the most memorable of all World Series games, dark clouds were hanging low over Boston and rain was threatening. Ruth got rid of the first two Brooklyn batters with dispatch but the third man, Hy Myers, a stocky righthanded-hitting outfielder, hit Babe's second pitch on a line to right centerfield. Centerfielder Tillie Walker tripped as he started after it and fell. Harry Hooper, coming over from rightfield, also stumbled, and the ball bounded through for extra bases. Hooper retrieved the ball near the fence and threw it in. The relay was bobbled and Myers, who never stopped running, beat the throw easily with a colorful but totally unnecessary headfirst slide into home plate. It was an inside-the-park home run, and it put Brooklyn ahead 1–0. It was

In front of the home fans in a home game but not at home, Ruth went 14 innings to beat Brooklyn in the World Series.

also the only run the Dodgers were to score in the game, which lasted 14 innings, although Brooklyn came very close a couple of times.

The Red Sox picked up a run in their half of the inning when Ruth grounded out, batting in a runner on third. The score was now 1–1, and it remained tied for 11 more innings. When the Red Sox came to bat in the last of the ninth, it was becoming dark, the gloom of the heavy overcast aggravated by the early October dusk. By the 11th inning, Ruth, who had difficulty earlier, looked stronger than ever. From the eighth inning on he allowed no hits at all and only one walk. Boston was oozing confidence and the Royal Rooters came to life. "Tessie!" they sang, and the band blared its accompaniment. Wilbert Robinson, the rotund Brooklyn manager, came red-faced and fuming off the Dodger bench and complained bitterly to the umpires, who dutifully ordered the

Royal Rooters to knock it off. In the 13th Mike Mowrey reached second for the Dodgers on an error and a sacrifice. Sherry Smith, a good hitting pitcher, poked a blooper into leftfield for what seemed a certain hit and an almost certain run. But Duffy Lewis came sprinting in and caught the ball off his shoe tops for the third out. You should have heard the Rooters sing *Tessie* then.

In the last of the 14th Smith, very tired, opened the inning by walking Dick Hoblitzell for the fourth time. Lewis sacrificed him to second. It was so dark now that it was hard to see the ball. Boston manager Bill Carrigan therefore put Del Gainor, a righthander, in to bat for the usually dependable Larry Gardner, who hit lefthanded, against the lefthanded Smith. Carrigan felt a righthand batter would be better able to follow Smith's pitches in the murky light. And using all his weapons, he sent slim young Mike McNally in to run for the heavy-footed Hoblitzell. Carrigan's maneuvers paid off. Gainor took a ball and a strike and then hit a liner over the third baseman's head. Most of the spectators could not tell where the ball went, but they could see Zack Wheat, the leftfielder, running desperately toward the foul line. McNally was around third before Wheat picked up the ball, and McNally scored easily with the winning run. Pandemonium. More *Tessie*. And Babe Ruth, in his World Series debut as a starter, had a 2–1, 14-inning victory in the longest World Series game ever played.

Ruth was roaring and shouting and jumping around the clubhouse afterwards like a high school kid. He grabbed Carrigan and yelled at him, "I told you a year ago I could take care of those National League bums, and you never gave me a chance." Carrigan, easing out of the Ruthian bear hug, laughed and said, "Forget it Babe. You made monkeys out of them today."

1917

>>>>>

. . . UNITED STATES DECLARES WAR ON GERMANY . . . FIRST PULITZER PRIZES ARE AWARDED IN LITERATURE . . . THE DIXIELAND JASS BAND MAKES FIRST JAZZ RECORDINGS . . .

JUNE 23

Starter Babe Ruth walks the first batter, yells at the ump and gets ejected. Ernie Shore (above, right) relieves, the base runner is thrown out trying to steal, and Shore retires the next 26 batters, resulting in an imperfect perfect game

1918

>>>>>

. . . SPANISH INFLUENZA KILLS A HALF MILLION AMERICANS . . . JACK DEMPSEY, FUTURE HEAVYWEIGHT CHAMP, FIGHTS 21 TIMES, GOES 19-1-1 . . . U.S. CONGRESS ESTABLISHES TIMES ZONES AND DAYLIGHT SAVINGS TIME . . .

APRIL 15

Team photo is taken at Fenway before Sox beat Philadelphia A's 7-1 to start the season. Baseball has a difficult summer as some question playing during wartime

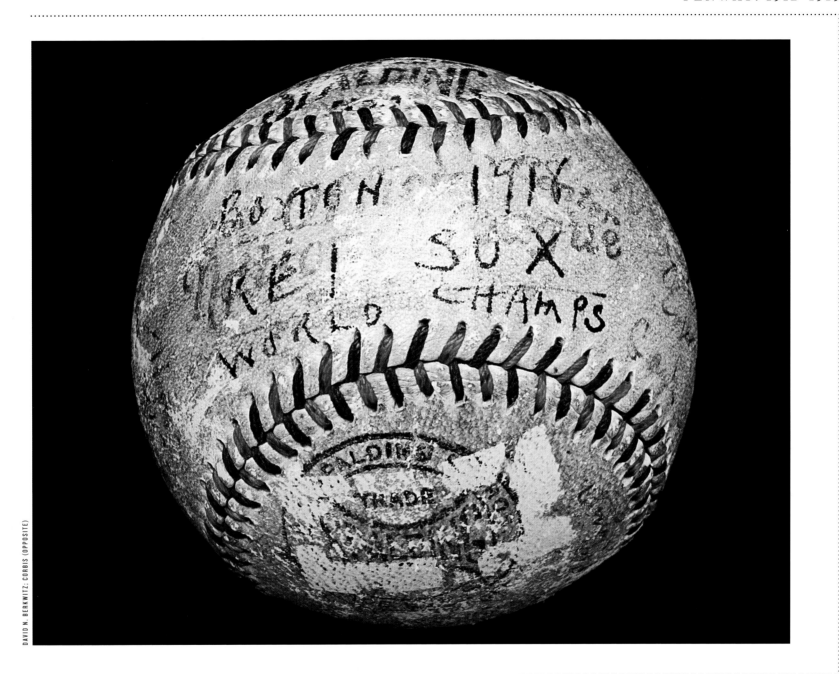

^
SEPTEMBER 11 ›

In a season cut short by war, the evening paper, and an autographed ball, proclaim the Red Sox world champs. Alas, the news won't be this good again for the Sox for 86 long years

‹ SEPTEMBER 11

Boston righty Carl Mays wins Game 6, after also winning Game 3, to clinch the World Series over the Chicago Cubs

LESLIE JONES COLLECTION/BOSTON PUBLIC LIBRARY PRINTS; MILO STEWART/NATIONAL BASEBALL HALL OF FAME

1919

>>>>>>

...*WHITE SOX PLAYERS, PAID BY GAMBLERS, THROW THE WORLD SERIES, ARE DUBBED BLACK SOX ...GREAT MOLASSES FLOOD KILLS 21 IN BOSTON...AMERICAN TELEPHONE AND TELEGRAPH INTRODUCES DIAL PHONES...*

JUNE 12 ›

Pitcher Herb Pennock, against the White Sox, faces the minimum 27 batters; he gives up three singles and a walk, but all four runners are erased on the basepaths

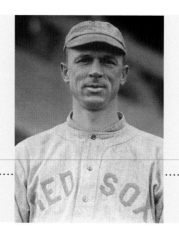

JUNE 29

A crowd of 50,000 packs Fenway at a rally for the Irish Republic, advocating Irish independence from the British

DECEMBER 26 ›

The Red Sox world is shaken to its core when owner Harry Frazee sells Babe Ruth to the Yankees. The Curse of the Bambino befalls Fenway

UNIFORM AGREEMENT
FOR TRANSFER OF A PLAYER

TO OR BY A
Major League Club

This Agreement, made and entered into this 26th day of December 1919

by and between Boston American League Baseball Club
(Party of the First Part)

and American League Base Ball Club of New York
(Party of the Second Part)

Witnesseth: The party of the first part does hereby release to the party of the second part the services of Player George H. Ruth under the following conditions:

(Here recite fully and clearly every condition of deal, including date of delivery; if for a money consideration, designate time and method of payment; if an exchange of players, name each; if option to recall is retained or privilege of choosing one or more players in lieu of one released is retained, specify all terms. No transfer will be held valid unless the consideration, receipt of which is acknowledged therein, passes at time of execution of Agreement.)

By herewith assigning to the party of the second part the contract of said player George H. Ruth for the seasons of 1919, 1920 and 1921, in consideration of the sum of Twenty-five Thousand ($25,000.) Dollars Cash and other good and valuable considerations paid by the party of the second part, receipt whereof is hereby acknowledged.

1920 TO 1929

Harry Frazee sells the Red Sox ~ Fire destroys
the leftfield grandstands ~ BU Terriers and
BC Eagles make Fenway their football home

April 1929
Red Sox trainer Bits Bierhalter stokes
the clubhouse stove as Boston players
warm up for an early season game.
Photograph by LESLIE JONES COLLECTION/
BOSTON PUBLIC LIBRARY PRINTS

1920

›››››

...THE AMERICAN PROFESSIONAL
FOOTBALL ASSOCIATION (APFA),
LATER TO BECOME THE NFL,
IS FOUNDED IN CANTON, OHIO
...19TH AMENDMENT GIVES
U.S. WOMEN RIGHT TO VOTE...
PROHIBITION IS INSTITUTED,
OUTLAWING ALCOHOLIC
BEVERAGES...

AUGUST 8 ›

John Philip Sousa leads
his Navy band in the first
ever concert at Fenway. His
Stars and Stripes Forever
inspires a five minute
standing ovation

1921

›››››

...WBZ BROADCASTS FIRST
COMMERCIAL RADIO PROGRAM
IN NEW ENGLAND...ITALIAN
IMMIGRANTS NICOLA SACCO AND
BARTOLOMEO VANZETTI ARE
ARRESTED, LATER EXECUTED FOR
MURDER...FIRST MISS AMERICA
PAGEANT HELD, IN ATLANTIC CITY...

^

DECEMBER 22

American League president
Ban Johnson (above) declines
to take action against Boston
owner Harry Frazee for selling
off Red Sox star players

BETTMANN/CORBIS (DUGAN); THE PROVIDENCE JOURNAL; LESLIE JONES COLLECTION/BOSTON PUBLIC LIBRARY PRINTS (OPPOSITE)

1922

>>>>>>

. . . SWIMMER JOHNNY WEISSMULLER
BREAKS THE ONE-MINUTE MARK
IN THE 100 METER FREESTYLE,
FINISHING IN 58.6 SECONDS . . .
U.S.S. "LANGLEY" IS COMMISSIONED
AS FIRST U.S. NAVAL AIRCRAFT
CARRIER . . . ARCHAEOLOGIST
HOWARD CARTER ENTERS KING
TUTANKHAMUN'S TOMB . . .

MAY 28 >

Irish Countess Constance
de Markievicz (far right),
speaking out against British
occupation of Ireland, is
cheered by a sympathetic
Fenway crowd made up
mostly of women

JULY 23

Infielder Joe Dugan
(above left) is unloaded by
Sox owner Harry Frazee
to the Yankees; the late
date of the lopsided trade
would prompt MLB to move
the next season's trade
deadline up to June 15. In
seven seasons with New
York, Dugan would return
often to Fenway (far left) as
the Yanks third baseman

AUGUST 14

Lizzie Murphy becomes the first
woman to play baseball at Fenway,
during a benefit game between the
Red Sox and an All-Star team

BOSTON RITUAL:
A STOP AT THIRD BASE

Nobody loved the Red Sox more than "Nuf Ced" McGreevy, and for baseball fans his saloon near Fenway was the place to be

HISTORY HAS NOW DEEMED it America's first sports bar. Its charismatic proprietor, Michael T. (Nuf Ced) McGreevy, opened his Boston saloon in 1894 on Columbus Avenue (later moving to Tremont Street) and named the place "Third Base Saloon," so dubbed because, as in baseball, it was the last place a man would visit on his way home. (His own moniker, Nuf Ced, rose from his habit of engaging his bar patrons in arguments about baseball; when, inevitably, he determined that he had proven himself right, McGreevy called out, " 'Nough said!")

From its earliest days, Third Base was the headquarters of the Royal Rooters fan club, with McGreevy its acknowledged leader; when Fenway opened in 1912, his tavern was but a 10-minute walk away, and continued to thrive. Over the years, Nuf Ced compiled an extraordinary collection of baseball memorabilia which decorated the walls of the saloon. Alas, when Prohibition hit, the bar, like so many others, was doomed; in 1920 McGreevy had to shut it down, but donated much his baseball collection to the Boston Public Library. Three years later, the library opened a new branch in the very building where Third Base had once been.

1923

＞＞＞＞＞＞

. . . YANKEE STADIUM OPENS IN THE BRONX . . . PRESIDENT WARREN G. HARDING DIES SUDDENLY, IS REPLACED BY FORMER MASSACHUSETTS GOVERNOR CALVIN COOLIDGE . . . BOSTON AIRPORT (NOW LOGAN) OPENS . . .

‹ MAY 10

The former site of the Third Base Saloon, famed tavern and social home of the Royal Rooters, becomes a branch of the Boston Public Library

‹ JULY 11

Harry Frazee (left) sells the Red Sox and Fenway Park for a little over $1 million to a group from the Midwest led by Bob Quinn who becomes new club president

‹ **AUGUST 9**

In Fenway's first Ladies Day game, Boston's Howard Ehmke pitches in a 4-3 Sox win over the Browns. At season's end, Ehmke will have 33% of the team's wins

SEPTEMBER 14 ›

Red Sox first baseman George Burns pulls off Fenway's first unassisted triple play; he catches a line drive by Cleveland's Frank Brower, tags Rube Lutzke between first and second, and beats Riggs Stephenson to the second base bag

1924

›››››

. . . BOSTON BRUINS ARE FOUNDED BY GROCERY TYCOON CHARLES ADAMS . . . CARDINALS SECOND BASEMAN ROGERS HORNSBY HITS .424, LAST PLAYER TO EXCEED .400 UNTIL TED WILLIAMS . . . COMPUTING TABULATING RECORDING CORPORATION (CTR) RENAMES ITSELF INTERNATIONAL BUSINESS MACHINES (IBM) . . .

^
APRIL 15

For a chilly opener, a well-bundled crowd turns out. Alas, the Sox lose 2-1 to the Yankees and, it seems, vendors (hot coffee?) are scarce

1925

››››››

...JOHN SCOPES IS ARRESTED IN TENNESSEE FOR TEACHING EVOLUTION THEORY...BOSTON ICON "OLD IRONSIDES" IS REFURBISHED, AND THE NAME U.S.S. CONSTITUTION IS RESTORED ...PETER DEPAOLO IS FIRST TO AVERAGE 100 MPH AT INDY 500...

^
NOVEMBER 14

In their first game using Fenway as their home field, the BU Terriers beat Providence College 14-6

1926

››››››

...ADMIRAL RICHARD BYRD CLAIMS TO BE FIRST TO FLY OVER NORTH POLE, A FEAT LATER DISPUTED...THE STANLEY CUP, ALREADY 34 YEARS OLD, BECOMES THE CHAMPIONSHIP TROPHY OF NHL...THE COLLEGE BOARD ADMINISTERS FIRST SAT EXAM...

SOX PARK HAS BLEACHER FIRE

Third Base Seats at Fenway Destroyed—Grand Stand Also Damaged—Blaze Caused by Burning Cigar or Cigarette —Breaks Out Shortly After Conclusion of Game

High Wind Shoots Flames All Through Structure—Many Volunteer Workers

Loss Is $25,000—Braves Field Offered Sox Management for Monday's Game

‹ MAY 8

A windblown fire, reportedly caused by trash ignited by a cigarette beneath the outfield bleachers, destroys the leftfield stands

MARK RUCKER/TRANSCENDENTAL GRAPHICS/GETTY IMAGES; UNDERWOOD & UNDERWOOD/CORBIS (OPPOSITE)

JUNE 24

The Sox beat the Yankees 6–5 on a quiet day at the plate for Babe Ruth. In a season in which he has 47 home runs, Ruth hits only two balls out of Fenway in 10 games there

AUGUST 21 ›

White Sox righty Ted Lyons throws a no-hitter in a 6-0 blanking of Boston. It will be the last no-hitter at Fenway for 30 years

1927

›››››

... CHARLES LINDBERGH MAKES FIRST SOLO TRANSATLANTIC FLIGHT... BOSTON MARATHON IS LENGTHENED TO 26 MILES, 365 YARDS TO CONFORM TO OLYMPICS STANDARDS... FIRST TALKING MOTION PICTURE, "THE JAZZ SINGER," IS RELEASED...

APRIL 21

Bill Carrigan returns to manage the Red Sox for the first time since leading them to the 1916 championship—but these Sox will finish last

‹ JUNE 23

Lou Gehrig is the first player to hit three home runs in a game at Fenway. The Yankees first baseman drives in five runs in New York's 11-4 win over Boston

75

Written for **SPORTS ILLUSTRATED 10.5.11**

BY AUSTIN MURPHY

THE YEAR OF THE EAGLES

Boston College, a football powerhouse in the 1920s, enjoyed its finest season in 1928, and most of the glory came on the makeshift gridiron of Fenway Park

THE BALL WAS LARGER, AS were the uniforms of the cheerleaders. Helmets lacked face masks, and the athletes wearing them played offense *and* defense. But college football in the 1920s and college football today hold certain things in common. Harvard despised Yale, and vice versa. Coaches loathed turnovers ("Better to have died a small boy than fumble this football," John Heisman told his charges at the start of each season.) And athletic directors wanted to maximize profits. Which is how the Boston College Eagles of 1928 and '29 found themselves playing home games five miles east of their Newton campus, at an oddly-configured, 16-year-old ballpark in the Fens section of the city.

The Eagles' on-campus stadium held scarcely 5,000 souls. In earlier years, games of note—which is to say, games that might yield bigger gates—had sometimes been moved to Fenway, but more often to Braves Field, home of the National League's Boston Braves. (That venue, long since demolished, is now the site of Boston University's Nickerson Field.)

The most notable of BC's Fenway moments had been a 17–14 win over Holy Cross in 1916, the Eagles' first victory in 17 years over their archrivals from Worcester. "As the shadows of eventide crept across the gridiron," wrote *The Boston Globe*'s Lawrence J. Sweeney, "[BC's] fondest hopes were realized."

But 1928 marked the first season that the Eagles would play *all* their home games at Fenway. Red Sox president Robert Quinn "has guaranteed the erection of 6,000 steel portable seats in both center and left field," the *Globe* announced on Aug. 2, 1928, "providing a total seating capacity of 35,000 for football games."

Boston College was coached by one Joseph McKenney, who'd been captain and quarterback of its undefeated (6-0-2) 1926 squad. That team had been coached by the Iron

McKenney, who'd quarterbacked BC to an undefeated season in '26, became their coach two years later, at 22.

Major, decorated war hero and head coach Frank Cavanaugh. But Cavanaugh had left for Fordham after the '26 season. Following the one-year tenure of D. Leo Daley, McKenney was a popular choice to take over the program. At 22, he was nation's youngest head coach, but that barely concerned the Eagles, or, for that matter, the local scribes: "Young in years, but wise in the ways of football," is how McKenney was described by the *Globe*'s Alfred J. Monahan. Alumni drew comfort from McKenney's knowledge of "the Cavanaugh system." Nor did it hurt that the roster was stocked with talent that Cavanaugh had recruited.

Of BC's nine games in 1928, seven were played at Fenway. The Eagles' toughest road test came in Annapolis on Oct. 7 when the visitors stunned heavily favored Navy 6–0. Coach McKenney found himself 5–0 as he prepared to

take on his mentor: On Nov. 12, Cavanaugh returned to Boston with his Fordham Rams. In a "dogged, stubborn battle" witnessed by 30,000 at Fenway, protégé beat mentor 19–7. The game's key play was a pick-six by Eagles left end John Dixon. Or, as the *Globe* put it, "Fordham made one fine overhead gain of 18 yards, but on the very next play a forward [pass] to the right lodged in Dixon's arms, and, absolutely uncovered . . . [he] raced down a clear field and scored." After that, we are told, "Fordham made small trouble" for the home team.

The Holy Cross Crusaders always meant trouble. The Eagles, now 8–0, were the last major undefeated team in the East. They'd been undefeated two years earlier, as well, when the Crusaders had stolen much of the season's luster, holding McKenney & Co. to a scoreless tie. Revenge was sweet: With its 19–0 victory over Holy Cross, BC clinched its second Eastern Championship in three years.

Twenty-eight years later, the Eagles would play their final game at Fenway—a desultory, 7–0 loss to Holy Cross. Red Sox owner Tom Yawkey had tired of renting the place out for football games, a decision that ushered Boston College to a crossroads. Its on-campus venue, Alumni Field, was still an underwhelming little structure, beneath the dignity of a major football power. Fordham and Georgetown had made the decisions, earlier in the decade, to downsize football. Would the Eagles as well?

"We could drop football," school president Joseph Maxwell said to William Flynn, the secretary of the alumni association who also happened to be an assistant football coach.

"Or we could build a stadium," replied Flynn.

The latter course was chosen, which is how it came to pass that a life-sized bronze statue of BC quarterback Doug Flutie was unveiled a few years ago outside gate D of Alumni Stadium—a facility now boasting some 7,000 more seats than Fenway Park.

1928

>>>>>

. . . BRUINS' NEW HOME ARENA
OPENS, CALLED BOSTON MADISON
SQUARE GARDEN . . . "IRON LUNG"
RESPIRATOR IS FIRST USED
AT BOSTON'S CHILDREN'S
HOSPITAL . . . MICKEY MOUSE
DEBUTS IN WALT DISNEY SHORT
"STEAMBOAT WILLIE" . . .

^
AUGUST 29

Jack Rothrock, a versatile Red Sox outfielder,
plays both third base and centerfield against the
St. Louis Browns. By season's end he will have
played all nine positions, including pitcher

1929

>>>>>

. . . NEW YORK STOCK EXCHANGE
CRASHES, MARKS START OF
GREAT DEPRESSION . . . BRUINS
CAPTURE STANLEY CUP OVER
NEW YORK RANGERS IN FIRST
ALL-U.S. FINALS . . . BOBBY
JONES WINS U.S. OPEN GOLF
TITLE IN 36-HOLE PLAYOFF BY 23
STROKES OVER AL ESPINOSA . . .

^
NOVEMBER 30

Boston College shuts down
chief rival Holy Cross 12-0 before
30,000; at game's end, the goal
posts are demolished by BC fans

<
APRIL 23

Governor Frank Allen throws out the first
ball at the Fenway opener. The Red Sox will
stumble to a 58-96 record, ending a woeful
decade without one winning season

77

SALE or RENT
ENTIRE BLDG. 12000 SQ FT.
FREIGHT ELEVATOR · RAILROAD SIDING
F. L. BUSWELL
73 TREMONT ST. BOSTON
CAPITOL 3856

January 5, 1934
Boston firemen fight a devastating blaze that began in the
bleachers during Fenway renovations. Amazingly, the ballpark
is ready, and better than ever, on Opening Day.
Photograph by LESLIE JONES COLLECTION/BOSTON PUBLIC LIBRARY PRINTS

1930
TO
1939

Boston Redskins bring pro football to Fenway ~
After fire, a new, higher wall rises in leftfield
~ Tom Yawkey buys team ~ Ted Williams debuts

1930

›››››

...SMOOT-HAWLEY ACT PUTS
LARGE TARIFF ON IMPORTED
GOODS, U.S. ECONOMY SINKS
FURTHER...URUGUAY HOSTS
AND WINS FIRST FIFA CUP...
CLARENCE BIRDSEYE INTRODUCES
FROZEN FOOD...

‹ JULY 2

Light-heavyweight
James J. Braddock
dominates Joe
Monte of Brockton
in a bout at Fenway;
Monte had won their
previous fight

1931

›››››

...NOTRE DAME COACH KNUTE
ROCKNE IS KILLED IN PLANE
CRASH...GANGSTER AL CAPONE
CONVICTED OF TAX EVASION,
SENTENCED TO PRISON..."THE
STAR-SPANGLED BANNER" IS MADE
OFFICIAL U.S. NATIONAL ANTHEM...

APRIL 22

Babe Ruth collapses in pain while
chasing a ball; he's carried from the
field by teammates and rushed to
Brigham Hospital with a severe cramp
in his left thigh. Ten days later he's back
in action; at June's end he's hitting .400

SEPTEMBER 12 ›

Tom Oliver drives in a run in the 13th to
beat Detroit. Starters Ed Durham and the
Tigers' Art Herring both pitch into the 13th
with shutouts, unique in Fenway history

Excerpted from SPORTS ILLUSTRATED 8.9.93

BY ROY BLOUNT JR.

THE DOUBLES CHAMP

An undistinguished and little-remembered Red Sox outfielder named Earl Webb set the major league season record for doubles, in 1931. Fluke or not, it's a record that still stands

IN 1931 EARL WEBB OF THE BOSTON Red Sox hit 67 doubles. No one else in major league history has ever hit more than 64. In this century only five players besides Webb, all of them now dead, have hit as many as 60 doubles. Only four players in the last 30 years have hit as many as 50. The closest anyone has come to threatening Webb's record since 1950 was Hal McRae when he hit 54 doubles with the Royals in 1977. As of this writing, John Olerud of the Toronto Blue Jays has 42 and is on a pace to catch Webb. Asked earlier to comment upon his pursuit of Webb's mark, the 25-year-old Olerud said he had never heard of Earl Webb or his mark.

So who is this Webb? And how do we account for the 67 doubles? When I first dug into this story, I figured the explanation was simple: Webb, a lefthanded hitter with moderate power, must have developed a patented swing, as they say, whereby he bounced a lot of ordinary fly balls off the Green Monster, Fenway's legendary leftfield wall. Many lefthanded-hitting Red Sox—Carl Yastrzemski, Fred Lynn and Wade Boggs spring to mind—have fattened their averages and their doubles totals by whapping the ball over to the opposite field.

But then I read this: "In 1931 the lefthanded-hitting Earl Webb hit a major league record 67 doubles. He never hit half as many in a season again and was a slow runner, but the record was not necessarily attributable to the dimensions of his home park: the Green Monster was not erected until 1934." I was thunderstruck. If the Green Monster wasn't responsible in 1931, what was?

What kind of a park was Webb's Fenway?

In fact, as I would learn, leftfield in Fenway was more doubleable in 1931 than it is now—for several reasons. The original wall, built in 1912, was itself a formidable structure and roughly only 320 feet from home plate; not only was the wall a handy target, but in front of it was an extraordinary hazard. The last 20 feet or so to the base of the wall was an

A variety of Fenway factors helped Webb set his record, but his feat failed to impress some Boston scribes.

embankment that sloped up about 10 feet and came to be known as Duffy's Cliff, because Sox leftfielder Duffy Lewis became so adept at playing it. "The secret was," in the recollection of Joe Cashman, who covered the Sox back then for Boston's *Daily Record*, "when the ball got out there, you had to be able to judge if it was catchable if you went up the cliff. If you got to the top and didn't catch it, the ball would hit the wall and bounce past you, and now you would have to run down and chase it halfway to the infield." What's more, when overflow crowds were sitting on the cliff, any ball hit into the spectators was a ground-rule double.

Other factors conspired to make 1931 a vintage year for two-baggers. After an explosion of offense in 1930, the ball was altered slightly in '31 to favor the pitchers; so it may well be that a number of balls Webb hit that would have been homers in '30 were doubles in '31. Also, 1931 was the first season in which balls that bounced over a fence were ruled doubles and not home runs.

And how about Fenway's centerfield and rightfield? For the largely nonpulling, lefthanded-hitting Webb, Fenway was a cavernous place: 388 feet to left center, 468 feet to dead center, a hard-to-believe 593 feet to the deepest corner just right of dead center. So there was lots and lots of room for Webb's drives to bounce and roll while he chugged into second.

Even if he had been faster, Webb probably would not have been tempted to stretch doubles into triples. He was in the right place at the right time to make history out of what, in today's parks, would probably be warning-track power—though some observers at the time seemed unimpressed. Indeed, the local press kept carping at Webb in '31 for being obsessed with the record—they called him the King of Dublin and accused him of turning triples into doubles. Clif Keane, the acknowledged dean of Boston baseball observers, recalled recently, "Outfielders would come tumbling down the cliff, and [Webb would] be jogging into second when he could've been on third. I'd say it happened at least 10 or 15 times." On the day Webb set the new mark, when he tied George Burns's then single-season record of 64 doubles in the first game of a doubleheader and broke it in the second, it was rated the fifth-biggest baseball story of Sept. 17 by the Associated Press. One Boston writer commended Webb offhandedly for his "stunt."

But let's give the man credit: He hit .333 that year and drove in 103 runs for a team that finished 45 games out of first place. Of his 67 doubles, 39 were hit in Fenway, 28 in other parks. So Webb would have had a heck of a doubles season even if he had been on the road all year. His home park, however, helped make him colossal.

1932

⟩⟩⟩⟩⟩⟩

. . . OWNER GEORGE PRESTON MARSHALL BRINGS NFL FRANCHISE TO BOSTON, KNOWN FIRST AS BRAVES, THEN REDSKINS . . . CHARLES LINDBERGH JR. IS KIDNAPPED, LATER FOUND DEAD . . . FIRST JACK BENNY RADIO SHOW IS BROADCAST . . .

ʌ
JULY 3

Sunday baseball is played at Fenway for the first time, after nearby Church of the Disciples withdraws its objections

ʌ
JULY 17

Boston pitchers Ed (Bull) Durham, Wilcy Moore, Bob Kline and Paul Ivy Andrews dress in the Fenway locker room before the Red Sox lose both ends of a doubleheader to Cleveland. The sad Sox will finish the season 43-111, worst in franchise history

ʌ
⟨ AUGUST 2

Light heavyweight champ Maxie Rosenbloom (left) beats Boston's Joe Barlow, winning all 10 rounds. Five weeks later at Fenway, Cuban junior lightweight Kid Chocolate also wins unanimously, over Steve Smith

1933

›››››

. . . 18TH AMENDMENT IS
REPEALED, ENDING PROHIBITION
IN U.S. . . . JIMMIE FOXX OF THE A'S
AND CHUCK KLEIN OF THE PHILLIES
EACH WIN THE TRIPLE CROWN
. . . FAY WRAY STARS IN FILM
"KING KONG" . . .

‹ **FEBRUARY 25**

New York industrialist and heir
Thomas Yawkey (left, with first
wife Elise) buys the woeful Red
Sox for $1.5 million and begins
repair of the badly worn Fenway

OCTOBER 8

The Boston Redskins, in their Fenway Park
debut and before 15,000 fans, nip the New
York Giants 21–20 on a blocked extra point.
The Redskins will play three more seasons at
Fenway before moving to Washington

JUNE 15

Yankees lose their fourth straight in Boston, and
angry Yanks owner Jacob Ruppert (above) calls in
the mortgage he's held on Fenway Park since 1920.
Red Sox owner Yawkey pays in full the next day

1934

›››››

. . . IN GOLF'S FIRST MASTERS
TOURNAMENT, HORTON SMITH
WINS BY ONE STROKE OVER CRAIG
WOOD . . . SUMNER TUNNEL
LINKING NORTH END TO EAST
BOSTON OPENS . . . SHIRLEY
TEMPLE MAKES SCREEN DEBUT IN
"BRIGHT EYES" . . .

˄ JANUARY 5

A fire starts in the new leftfield bleachers, sparked by workers making renovations. The five-alarm blaze does massive damage, not only to Fenway but to other enterprises on Lansdowne Street

˄ APRIL 17

Following the '33 season, Tom Yawkey decides to level Duffy's Cliff in leftfield. For the '34 season opener, the famed embankment is gone

‹ JANUARY 31

Repairs after the fire move swiftly thanks to 950 workers; when completed, in time to start the '34 season, leftfield will feature a new 37-foot high fence and the entire park will be repainted in a color known then as "Dartmouth green"

KING OF THE HILL

Boston outfielder Duffy Lewis could play the game, no doubt, but it's fair to say he'd be barely remembered if not for one special skill

UP AND DOWN HE'D GO ON that hill, chasing batted balls with such grace and efficiency that, eventually, they went ahead and named the darn thing after him. Red Sox leftfielder Duffy Lewis, a scrappy .289 hitter with Boston from 1910 to '17, became a master at playing balls off the awkward 10-foot grass embankment that angled upward against the towering wall that stretched from the leftfield foul pole to center. "Duffy's Cliff" had two purposes when built: It provided a support base for the 25-foot wall and it compensated for the differential in land grades between field level and that of Lansdowne Street, bordering the park to the north. On days when Fenway saw an overflow crowd, the grassy hill would be roped off and become a prime spot for fans to sit. (A ball hit into the crowd became a ground-rule double.)

When the park was refurbished by new owner Tom Yawkey in 1934, Duffy's Cliff was leveled. Now when a leftfielder is positioned at the Wall, he stands about seven feet below Lansdowne Street—which, some surmise, accounts for the occasional rat that visits the scorekeepers inside the Green Monster.

1935

››››››

. . . SUFFOLK DOWNS RACETRACK OPENS IN EAST BOSTON . . . BABE RUTH JOINS BRAVES, HITS THREE HOMERS IN A GAME HIS LAST ACTIVE WEEK . . . SOCIAL SECURITY ACT ESTABLISHES RETIREMENT INSURANCE . . .

‹ **APRIL 14**

In his last appearance at Fenway as a player, now a Boston Brave, Babe Ruth and teammates beat the Red Sox in an exhibition game, 3-2

^
APRIL 23

New shortstop and manager Joe Cronin debuts in the Fenway opener; he will serve as Boston player-manager for 11 seasons, making five All-Star teams

1936

›››››

...JESSE OWENS WINS FOUR GOLD MEDALS AT THE BERLIN OLYMPICS ...BOSTON'S MUSEUM OF FINE ARTS IS FOUNDED...HENRY LUCE PUBLISHES FIRST ISSUE OF "LIFE" MAGAZINE...

APRIL 14

The '36 Red Sox were comfortable at home, compiling a 47–29 record at Fenway. Unfortunately, a 27–51 road record doomed them to a sixth-place finish

1937

›››››

...GERMAN ZEPPELIN "HINDENBURG" EXPLODES OVER NEW JERSEY...RACEHORSE WAR ADMIRAL WINS TRIPLE CROWN... NEW FABRIC, NYLON, IS PATENTED BY DUPONT...

‹ **JUNE 11**

The Boston brother battery of pitcher Wes Farrell (far left) and catcher Rick Farrell is traded, in tandem, to Washington

JUNE 20 ›

With a packed house for a Sunday doubleheader against Cleveland, fans took roost in the outfield billboard supports

SEPTEMBER 27

Fenway fans saw Sox slugger Jimmie
Foxx in his prime in '37, when he hit 37
home runs, two of them on this day. The
next season he would be even better,
with 50 dingers and his third MVP

‹ SEPTEMBER 11

Reigning Heisman winner, end
Larry Kelley of Yale, and a team
of college all-stars fall to the
Washington Redskins 30-27

1938

››››››

*. . . FREAK HURRICANE, FIRST
IN NEW ENGLAND SINCE 1869,
KILLS HUNDREDS . . . DON BUDGE
IS FIRST TO COMPLETE SINGLES
GRAND SLAM OF TENNIS . . .
RADIO BROADCAST OF ORSON
WELLES'S "WAR OF THE WORLD"
INCITES PANIC . . .*

MAY 3 ›

Lefty Grove goes 10
innings to beat the
Tigers 4-3. It begins his
streak of 20 consecutive
wins at Fenway

^

SEPTEMBER 14

The Pittsburgh Pirates (later the Steelers), featuring Byron "Whizzer" White (later a Supreme Court Justice), beat the Boston Shamrocks 16-6. The Shamrocks would go out of business at season's end

1939

〉〉〉〉〉〉

. . . GERMANY INVADES POLAND, BEGINS WORLD WAR II . . . IN FIRST NCAA BASKETBALL TOURNAMENT, OREGON BEATS OHIO STATE IN FINAL . . . AT NEW YORK WORLD'S FAIR, DEVICE CALLED TELEVISION IS FIRST EXHIBITED . . .

〈 APRIL 21

Rookie Ted Williams makes his regular-season Fenway debut, against the A's. The Kid gets his first hit (a single) and his first RBI

1940
TO
1949

Notre Dame's No. 1 football team routs Dartmouth ~ Ted
Williams hits longest Fenway homer ~ Red Sox fall to
Cardinals in '46 Series ~ The lights come on at Fenway

November 12, 1949
The Boston University Terriers, who call Fenway home for 28 seasons, fall to St. Bonaventure in the '49 finale, 19–0.

Photograph by LESLIE JONES COLLECTION/BOSTON PUBLIC LIBRARY PRINTS

FOR LOVE OF A LOGO

A sign went up in 1940 and never really came down. It may be the country's most cherished billboard

FROM JUST ABOUT ANY SEAT it can be seen, as much a part of the iconography of Fenway as any other feature of the park: the Citgo sign. In 1940, the Cities Service Company, a petroleum producer founded 30 years earlier, hoisted the company's sign over its divisional office at 600 Beacon Street in Kenmore Square, just north of Fenway. Whether by crafty commercial intent or happy luck, the sign happened to stand in full view above the park's leftfield wall, about 1,200 feet from home plate; featuring the company's green and white "trefoil" logo, it could not be missed. In June of 1965, after a corporate name change to Citgo, a new sign arose with the orange "trimark" logo. Fans noted that this version was indeed more fitting, offering a SEE-IT-GO salute to home runs sailing in its direction.

The sign has endured a shutdown for "energy conservation" in the '70s, a threatened dismantling until saved by protestors in the '80s, a techno-overhaul in 2005 and even a damaging fire in '08. The present day sign, said to be the largest in New England, measures 60 × 60 feet. Its most recent renovation was completed in '10, the relighting neatly coinciding with the 100th anniversary of Cities Service.

COURTESY OF CITGO PETROLEUM CORPORATION; J. WALTER GREEN/AP (OPPOSITE)

1940

〉〉〉〉〉〉

. . . BEARS CRUSH THE REDSKINS 73–0 IN NFL TITLE GAME, MOST LOPSIDED EVER . . . IGOR SIKORSKY DEMONSTRATES FIRST HELICOPTER . . . McDONALD BROTHERS OPEN FIRST McDONALD'S RESTAURANT, IN SAN BERNARDINO, CALIF., OFFERING 15-CENT HAMBURGERS . . .

AUGUST 17

A Cities Service sign, with the company's green and white logo, is erected near Fenway and is visible to fans, beyond leftfield

AUGUST 24

With the Sox losing 11–1 to the Tigers, Ted Williams makes his major league pitching debut. The righty Williams goes two innings giving up a run on three hits; in his finest moment, he strikes out slugger Rudy York on three pitches

SEPTEMBER 10 〉

Slingin' Sammy Baugh, quarterback of the Washington Redskins, throws three touchdown passes in a preseason exhibition against a team of college All Stars. A crowd of 26,000 sees the 'Skins win 35–12

NOVEMBER 30

BC 7, Holy Cross 0: the Eagles
complete an unbeaten football
season and win the Lambert
Trophy as top team in the East

1941

>>>>>

*...JAPAN ATTACKS PEARL
HARBOR... BRUINS, LED BY
THE "KRAUT LINE," WIN SECOND
STANLEY CUP IN THREE YEARS...
LES PAUL CREATES FIRST SOLID-
BODY ELECTRIC GUITAR...*

JULY 25

Lefty Grove wins his 300th
game, going nine innings and
beating the Indians 10-6; it will
be his last career win

SEPTEMBER 1 ›

Williams appears on the cover of
LIFE magazine (coverline: NO. 1 BATTER)
on his way to hitting .406; at Fenway
that season, he hit .428

SEPTEMBER 9

Big day for young Dom
DiMaggio (sliding into
third in the fourth inning);
he has a grand slam, a
triple and a double and, in
combination with Sox ace
Dick Newsome's 4-hitter,
trounces the Tigers 6-0

93

1942

〉〉〉〉〉

...FIRE AT BOSTON'S COCOANUT GROVE NIGHTCLUB KILLS 492... FDR ENCOURAGES MAJOR LEAGUE BASEBALL TO OPERATE DURING WORLD WAR II FOR NATIONAL MORALE...MOTION PICTURE "CASABLANCA" STARRING HUMPHREY BOGART PREMIERES...

^

AUGUST 19

Red Sox ace Tex Hughson beats the Yankees 6–4 for his eighth consecutive victory

^

AUGUST 27

Dinny Glynn wins a pregame baserunning contest, then the kid gets a few hitting tips from The Kid (who later in the day hits his 27th home run)

^

SEPTEMBER 3

After allegedly hurling his bat at a pigeon during batting practice, Williams climbs the screen to retrieve his weapon

NOVEMBER 28

No. 1 Boston College loses 55–12 to Holy Cross in a blizzard, but there is a fateful silver lining: the BC team's planned victory party at the Cocoanut Grove is canceled after the loss; it is the night the club burns down in the catastrophic fire

⌄

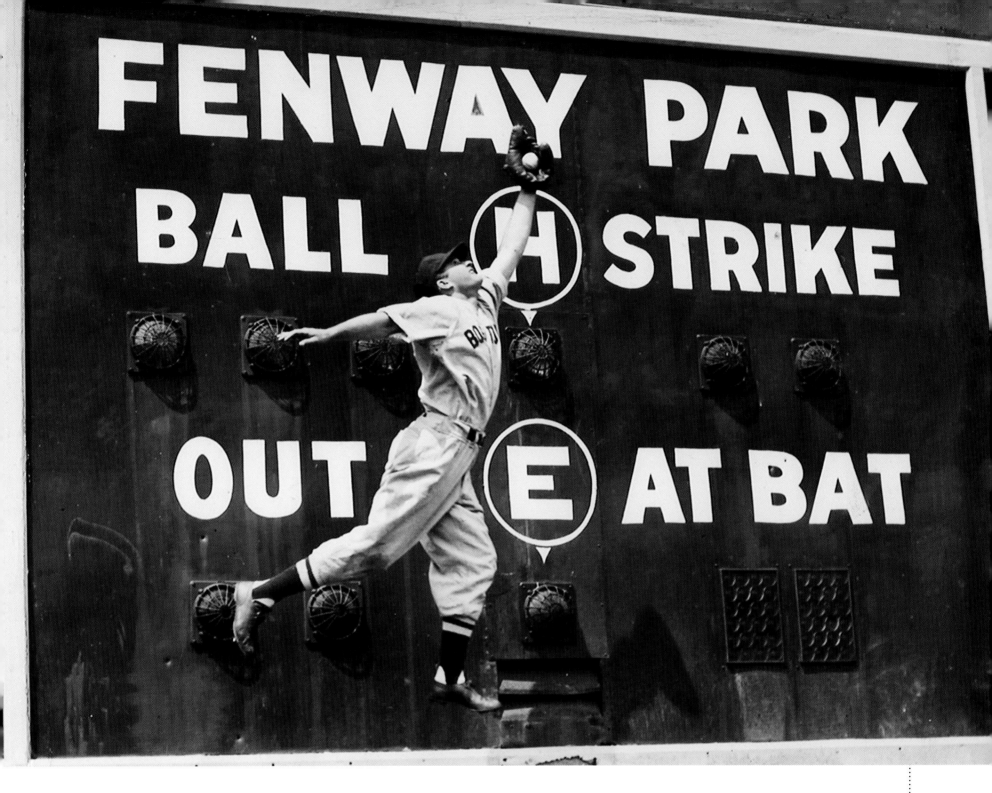

1943

>>>>>>

...NFL MAKES HELMETS MANDATORY FOR ALL PLAYERS... U.S. GOVERNMENT INTRODUCES WITHHOLDING OF FEDERAL INCOME TAX FROM WAGES... RODGERS AND HAMMERSTEIN MUSICAL "OKLAHOMA!" OPENS ON BROADWAY...

MAY 21

On his first day at Fenway as a Red Sox outfielder, rookie Leon Culberson leaps high against the leftfield scoreboard for a spectacular . . . promotional photo

JULY 12

Williams and Babe Ruth duel for the upper hand at Fenway before the start of a hitting contest on Mayor's Field Day

AUGUST 29

The Stadium Circus comes to Fenway, with appearances by celebrities such as swimmer and film star Buster Crabbe

1944

>>>>>

. . . ALLIED FORCES INVADE
NORMANDY COAST IN FRANCE . . .
ARMY FOOTBALL TEAM WINS FIRST
OF THREE STRAIGHT NATIONAL
CHAMPIONSHIPS . . . BIG-BAND
LEADER, AND ARMY AIR FORCE
MAJOR, GLENN MILLER IS PRESUMED
DEAD AFTER HIS PLANE VANISHES
OVER ENGLISH CHANNEL . . .

OCTOBER 14 >

In Notre Dame's
first and only visit to
Fenway, the No. 1-
ranked Fighting Irish,
behind quarterback
Johnny Lujack, pound
Dartmouth 64-0

NOVEMBER 4

President Franklin D. Roosevelt
addresses a Fenway crowd of
40,000 in what will be the final
campaign speech of his career.
Three days later he wins reelection,
beating Republican Thomas Dewey

1945

>>>>>

. . . U.S. DROPS ATOMIC BOMBS
IN JAPAN; WORLD WAR II ENDS
. . . ONE-ARMED OUTFIELDER
PETE GRAY PLAYS 77 GAMES FOR
ST. LOUIS BROWNS . . . WORLD'S
FIRST DIGITAL COMPUTER, ENIAC,
IS COMPLETED AT UNIVERSITY OF
PENNSYLVANIA . . .

APRIL 16

The Red Sox bring in Negro leaguer
Jackie Robinson for a tryout. He peppers the leftfield wall with batted balls, but he is not signed by Boston

MAY 6

Rookie Dave (Boo) Ferris makes his Fenway debut with a 5-0 shutout of the Yankees. In '46, he will go 13-0 at Fenway

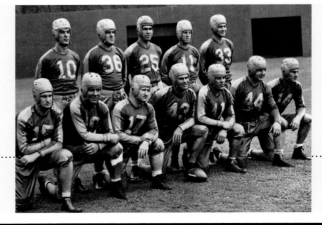

NOVEMBER 4

The Boston Yanks, in their second of five NFL seasons at Fenway, fall to the Detroit Lions 10-9 in a snowstorm

TIME TO TRY
TYDOL
GASOLINE
NEW
GIANT POWER

1946

›››››

...BOSTON CELTICS ARE FORMED
AND JOIN THE BASKETBALL
ASSOCIATION OF AMERICA...
UNITED NATIONS GENERAL
ASSEMBLY MEETS FOR FIRST TIME
...DR. BENJAMIN SPOCK'S BOOK
"BABY AND CHILD CARE"
IS PUBLISHED...

APRIL 14

A crowd of 33,279 packs
Fenway for the final playing
of the Boston Red Sox–
Boston Braves exhibition
series. The Sox win 19-5

‹ APRIL 30

John F. Kennedy, age 28 and
campaigning for a House
seat, visits Fenway, and
chats with Tigers outfielder
Hank Greenberg

JUNE 9 ›

Ted Williams hits a 502-foot
home run, longest in Fenway
history. In 1983, seat 21, row
37, section 42—where the ball
landed—will be painted red

AP (2)

JULY 9 ›

At the All-Star game, Sox DiMaggio, York and Williams pose with Ken Keltner. Williams has two homers and five RBIs in a 12–0 AL rout

OCTOBER 9

In the first inning of Game 3 of the World Series, with two outs and a runner on second, Cardinals catcher Joe Garagiola takes no chances as Ted Williams is intentionally walked. The next batter, Rudy York, hits a three-run homer. Boston will win 4–0

OCTOBER 9

Cardinal Stan Musial gets picked off second and run down by Pinky Higgins and pitcher Boo Ferriss; Game 3 is Fenway's first World Series game in 28 years

1947

›››››

. . . HOLY CROSS, WITH FRESHMAN BOB COUSY, WINS NCAA BASKETBALL TOURNAMENT . . . JACKIE ROBINSON PLAYS FOR BROOKLYN DODGERS, BREAKS BASEBALL COLOR BARRIER . . . JOHN HANCOCK BUILDING IN BACK BAY IS COMPLETED . . .

‹ APRIL 15

The season opens with a new look in left; all signage has been removed from the wall, now painted green

JUNE 13 ›

The new lights debut in Fenway's first night game. The Red Sox adjust, beat the White Sox 5–3

Leigh Montville is the author of **TED WILLIAMS:** THE BIOGRAPHY OF AN AMERICAN HERO

BY LEIGH MONTVILLE

AN UNCOMFORTABLE HOME

Despite attempts to make Fenway more friendly to Ted Williams, the park never fully suited his game or his temperament. The only thing he clearly liked was the abundance of pigeons

THERE WERE NO OFF DAYS for the batboys. The salary was $2 per game, flat rate, but the duties were stretched across the summer months of the 1949 calendar. An off day for the Red Sox meant an unpaid afternoon of shining shoes, running errands, cleaning floors, doing whatever had to be done in the Sox clubhouse at Fenway Park.

On this particular off day, as 15-year-old George Sullivan of Cambridge, Mass., hurried to his chores, arriving outside Fenway and late for work, he was surprised to hear a series of explosions from inside the park's brick walls. Explosions?

Probably a backfire, he decided to himself, as he slipped inside a service gate.

Or probably a beer truck, he decided further, the explosions louder now as he climbed a ramp toward the field.

Or probably . . .

He couldn't believe what he saw in front of him.

Probably . . . Ted Williams?

Ted Williams, shooting pigeons.

The 30-year-old slugger, the most famous, most controversial man in Boston, the local all-time star of stars, was in the rightfield Red Sox bullpen with his rifle. *Blam*. He fired across the field at the pigeons. *Blam*. The sound echoed around the ballpark, louder than the crack of any bat against a baseball. *Blam*. The pigeons fell from the big-city sky, landing like so many pop flies in the leftfield grass.

"Hey, buddy," the great man said, later in the afternoon, putting his arm around George Sullivan's shoulders in the clubhouse. "Do me a favor. Go out and pick up those birds for me, will ya?"

Sullivan filled three garbage cans with dead birds. The blood, the guts, the feathers, seemed to be everywhere. Yuck. What a job. What next?

There were no off days for batboys. Especially when Ted Williams was around.

It was not as unusual as it should have been to see Williams at Fenway not with a bat in hand but a rifle.

"I studied him every day of that summer," Sullivan said more than 50 years later, the memories still as fresh as the day they were made. "I was fascinated by him. Everybody was. I'd see it when he came into the clubhouse. Everything changed. His teammates were as in awe of him as I was. Conversations would stop or switch to whatever he was talking about. He had that big voice. He was in control."

For the entire decade of the Forties, except for the necessary interruption for World War II in the middle, Fenway Park was the playground, the home, the perpetual public stage for this oversized and quirky character from San Diego. Ted Williams was loved. He was hated. He was never ignored. Public opinion about him could change by the day, hour, next at bat. He preened and pouted. He swore a continual blue streak as he hit baseballs at a staggering rate of success. He feuded daily with the reporters of the many local newspapers. He lived the life of a tortured artist.

His ears were fine-tuned to hear negativity. That was how he worked. If 10,000 people cheered his name and one person made a wise remark, the remark was what was remembered. Don't think Theodore Samuel Williams can do it, huh? Think I'm a bum, huh? Well, I WILL SHOW YOU. Success usually was accompanied by the sound of grinding teeth.

"I went to a game with my wife at Fenway," Max West, an outfielder with the Boston Braves in 1940, said. "I was injured, couldn't make a road trip with the Braves, was going out of my mind. I said, 'Hey, let's go see Ted.' We had good seats behind the visitors dugout at Fenway, on the leftfield line."

West spotted trouble quickly. A large man with a beer belly and a loud voice started yelling at Williams early in the game. Every time Williams came in from the field, he ran closer and closer to the line and stared at the man with the beer belly and the loud voice.

"Watch this," Max West told his wife. "Something's going to happen here."

Sure enough. Williams stopped in the middle of one of his trips to the dugout. He pointed at the beer belly.

"You," he said.

"You know who you are," he said.

"You're a son of a bitch."

That was part of a Fenway day with Ted.

The awkward dance between star and patrons had begun in 1940. His rookie season, '39, was fine, terrific for a 20-year-old kid, a .327 average, 31 home runs, a league-leading

145 RBIs He finished fourth in the MVP voting. There were no histrionics. He tipped his cap at the sound of applause.

In 1940, alas, the Red Sox tried to make a good thing better.

The team added home and visiting bullpens in rightfield, bringing the fences in 20 feet to help their lefthanded-hitting phenom hit more home runs. The bullpens, which reduced the distance in the power alley from 400 feet to 380 feet, were immediately called "Williamsburg." Williams's spot in the Boston batting order also was changed for the 1940 season as he moved from cleanup to third, flip-flopping with slugger Jimmie Foxx. This was an effort to force pitchers to pitch to Williams, wary of Foxx hitting behind him in the cleanup spot. A final change was made, to Williams's position in the field. He was switched from right, the expansive sun field, to left, a tighter, easier place to play.

All of this, done for a 21-year-old kid, seemed to the Boston sporting populace to be a bit premature. Maybe he should have to put together two seasons, three . . . there was a sense of favoritism here that did not land well with the public.

The first boos were heard at a Fenway exhibition game. As the '40 season progressed, it was obvious that the bullpen addition didn't help—Williams's home runs tended to be hit on a line that carried across the bullpens of Williamsburg anyway, and now the frequency of his homers was declining as he began to press. And as the boos continued, he made some strange comments.

First, he said that he was going to quit baseball and become a fireman. He had an uncle

> ## 66 For Williams every day at Fenway was a battle. He would never love the place, never see the charm in it. The intimacies of the park were annoyances. 99

who had been a fireman in Mount Vernon, N.Y., and that seemed to him like a much better life, a much better job than leftfielder for the Red Sox. Second, he declared how much he hated the city of Boston. He hated the fans, he hated the newspapers, hated the trees, the weather, the streets, the way the houses were built. This was a young man's frustrations in control—he also wanted a new contract—but the people in the city he said he hated were not amused.

"The lad is a high-strung nerve victim who thinks whole headfuls of thoughts at a time in a cerebral chop suey instead of single ideas in a sequence like little pork sausages," Austin Lake, one of the hated columnists, wrote in the *Boston American*. "Big money, quick fame, mass adulation, a celebrity at 22, have fogged his perspective."

The battle had begun. It would last for the rest of Williams' cantankerous 21-year career in a Red Sox uniform. He would spit, fume, hit .406 in 1941, struggle in the '46 World Series, on and on, every day at Fenway a battle.

He never would love the place, never would see any charm in it. He thought the park worked against him as a hitter with its deep rightfield. (The imagined megatrade of the day always

sent Williams to New York for Joe DiMaggio, the lefthand-hitting Williams more content at Yankee Stadium with its short rightfield, the righthanded DiMaggio better at Fenway with its short field in left.) The intimacies of the park were annoyances. He could hear the negative voices too well. He could react too quickly.

"He also could be very nice," George Sullivan said. "He would give me a ride home sometimes. He had two cars, a Cadillac and a Ford. He'd drop me off at my corner, Kerry Corner, right in front of the Varsity Spa, where everybody could see. I was the kid who got a ride home from Ted Williams."

Years later, eight seasons after young George found Williams shooting birds, there would be another, more famous incident at Fenway with the slugger and pigeons and a rifle—reporters spotting the target practice, stories written, the Humane Society soon involved, headlines everywhere—but Sullivan was not involved in that. The 1949 season was his lone season as a batboy.

"I grew too tall in the off-season," he said. "I was over six feet when I came back. I was taller than some of the players. That didn't look good. So I was out of a job."

1948

>>>>>>

. . .BOSTON BRAVES FALL TO CLEVELAND IN WORLD SERIES . . . EDDIE ARCARO RIDES CITATION TO HORSE RACING TRIPLE CROWN, ARCARO'S SECOND AFTER WINNING ON WHIRLAWAY IN '41 . . . WBZ-BOSTON IS FIRST TV STATION ON AIR IN NEW ENGLAND . . .

⟨ **OCTOBER 4**

In a one-game playoff for the American League pennant after finishing the season tied, the Indians beat the Red Sox 8-3, and celebrate by carrying off winning pitcher Gene Bearden

1949

>>>>>>

. . .MAO TSE-TUNG FOUNDS PEOPLE'S REPUBLIC OF CHINA . . . NBL AND BAA MERGE TO FORM NATIONAL BASKETBALL ASSOCIATION . . .FIRST EMMYS ARE AWARDED BY ACADEMY OF TELEVISION ARTS AND SCIENCES; SHIRLEY DINSDALE WINS BEST TV PERSONALITY . . .

^

NOVEMBER 12

BU is beaten 14–13 in football by Maryland; calling his debut game for CBS radio is a young broadcaster named Vin Scully

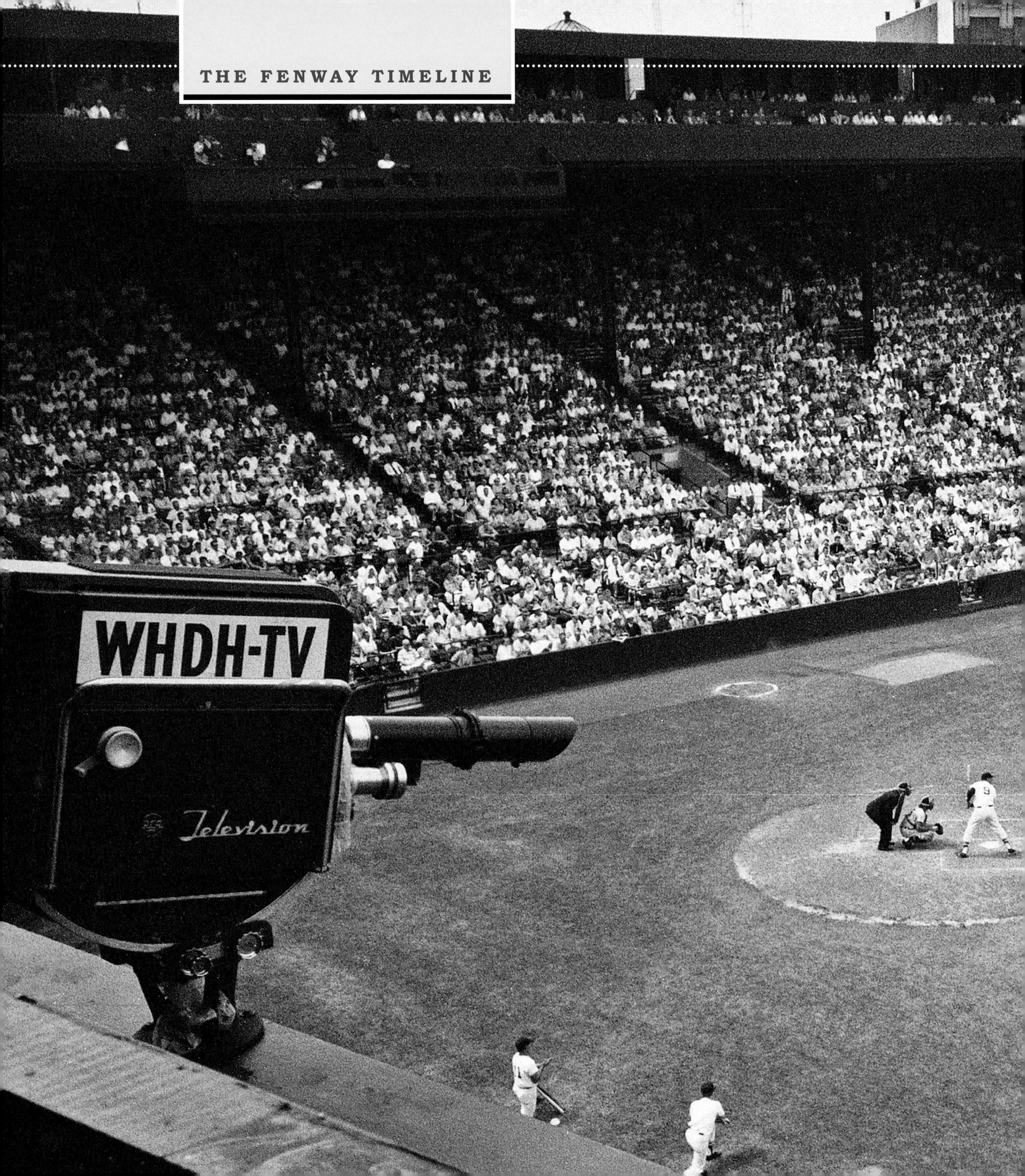
WHDH-TV
Television

1950
TO
1959

SYLVANIA TV

Ted Williams leaves to serve in Korean War ~ Local boy Harry Agganis pulls off a football/baseball combo on the Fenway turf ~ Jimmy Piersall writes a book

July 19, 1958
With TV cameras now a Fenway fixture, Williams bats against Detroit; his 12th-inning homer wins it for the Sox.
Photograph by JAMES F. COYNE

1950

>>>>>>

...BRINK'S ROBBERY IN BOSTON NETS 11-MEMBER GANG $3 MILLION ...BEN HOGAN WINS U.S. OPEN AFTER RECOVERY FROM AUTO ACCIDENT...DUNKIN' DONUTS IS FOUNDED IN QUINCY, MASS....

FEBRUARY 7 ›

Manager Joe Cronin invites Ted Williams to his office to sign baseball's richest contract ever, in excess of $120,000

^ APRIL 18

Before the season opener at Fenway, the game's two biggest stars, Williams and Joe DiMaggio, strike a pose. The irascible Williams, perhaps with his new contract in mind, wears a rare big smile

AMERICAN LEAGUE

P		1	2	3	4	5	6	7	8	9	H
24	ST. LOUIS	0	0	3	0	0	0	0	0	0	6
22	BOSTON	0	8	5	7	2	0	2	5		28
	DETROIT										
	NEW YORK					N	I	T	E		

‹ **JUNE 8**

Bobby Doerr hits three home runs in a 29-4 drubbing of the St. Louis Browns, the most runs scored by the Red Sox in their history. Williams (above) admires the results, including 28 Boston hits

‹ **JUNE 11**

Johnny Pesky hits a home run just inside the rightfield foul pole, which stands only 302 feet from home plate. It will later be dubbed the Pesky Pole (he hit only six Fenway home runs his entire career) by Red Sox broadcaster and former pitcher Mel Parnell

1951

›››››

. . . FIRST NBA ALL-STAR GAME IS PLAYED, IN BOSTON GARDEN . . . "I LOVE LUCY" DEBUTS ON CBS TELEVISION . . . BOSTON MUSEUM OF SCIENCE OPENS ON CHARLES RIVER . . .

^
MAY 15

Cy Young, the game's winningest pitcher, appears at Fenway in celebration of baseball's golden anniversary

A RARE DOUBLE PLAY

Hometown hero Harry Agganis made two-sport history at Fenway

THEY CALLED HIM "THE Golden Greek" and he had few athletic peers in his tragically short life. Harry Agganis, a native of Lynn, Mass., was a dual-sport star in football and baseball, first at Lynn Classical High, then at Boston University. He also played both sports for the Marines at Camp Lejeune (N.C.), and in 1951, Agganis pulled off what is surely a unique trick in Fenway history. In June he played first base for the Camp Lejeune baseball team, helping them to beat Boston College in a game at Fenway. In October, having left the Marines to return to Boston to care for his ailing mother, Agganis played quarterback for BU, and, again at Fenway, beat his old Camp Lejeune football team.

His record-setting football career at BU earned him a $25,000 offer to play for the Cleveland Browns. Red Sox owner Tom Yawkey, however, outbid the Browns, offering Agganis $35,000 to play baseball instead. In '54, his first season with the Red Sox, Agganis hit 11 home runs, but played just 25 games in '55 before being hospitalized with pneumonia.

The local golden boy died on June 27, 1955, of a pulmonary embolism, at the age of 26, leaving Boston fans in shock and mourning. Ten thousand attended his funeral.

AP (2)

OCTOBER 13

The Boston University football team, led by quarterback and local hero Harry Agganis, entertains the Fenway crowd with a 16-0 whipping of Camp Lejeune, a U.S. Marines team

1952

››››››

... DWIGHT EISENHOWER DEFEATS ADLAI STEVENSON IN PRESIDENTIAL ELECTION ... JOHN F. KENNEDY WINS U.S. SENATE SEAT OVER HENRY CABOT LODGE ... USSR MAKES OLYMPIC DEBUT IN HELSINKI ...

APRIL 13

The Boston Braves play their last game at Fenway Park. A former Fenway tenant, the Braves are the visiting team in the City Series exhibition against the Red Sox. The next season they will move to Milwaukee

APRIL 30 ›

Williams is presented with a Cadillac, then cleans out his locker before reporting to the Marines for duty in Korea

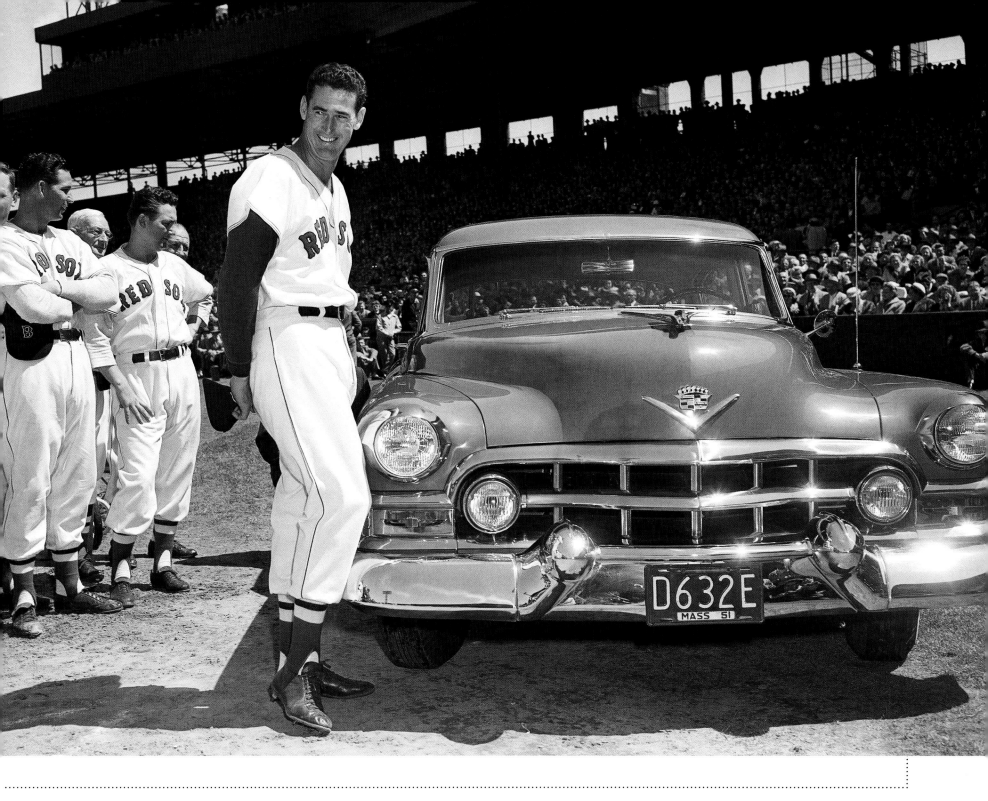

< JUNE 4

Larry Doby, the first
black player in the
American League, hits for
the cycle, but his Indians
lose to the Sox 13–11

1953

>>>>>>

...SIR EDMUND HILLARY
REACHES SUMMIT OF MOUNT
EVEREST...ETHEL AND JULIUS
ROSENBERG ARE EXECUTED FOR
ESPIONAGE...JONAS SALK
UNVEILS POLIO VACCINE...

< APRIL 14

Pitcher Mel Parnell hurls
snowballs instead of fastballs
as Opening Day at Fenway is
postponed by a freak storm

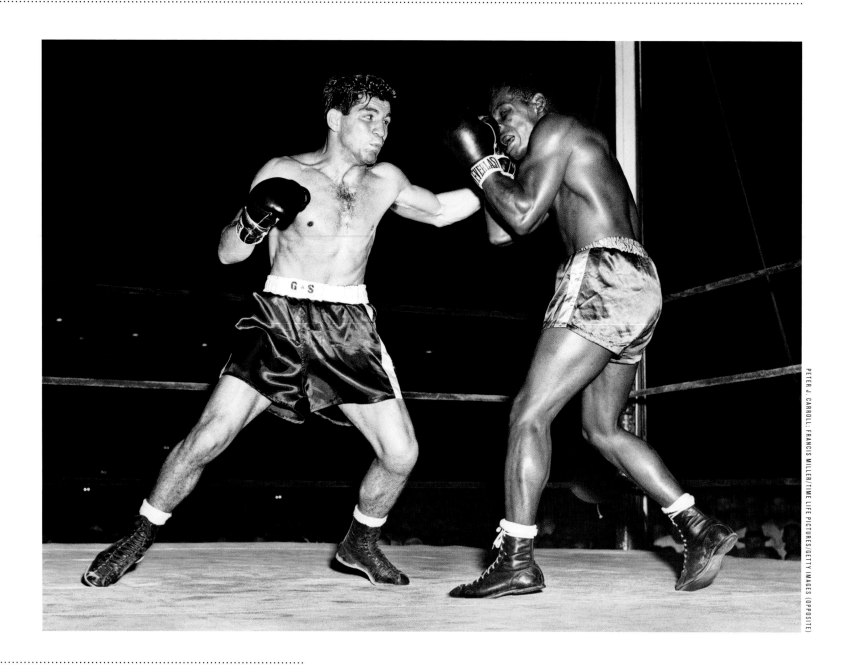

PETER J. CARROLL; FRANCIS MILLER/TIME LIFE PICTURES/GETTY IMAGES (OPPOSITE)

1954

>>>>>>

. . . ROGER BANNISTER RUNS FIRST
FOUR-MINUTE MILE . . . BILL HALEY
AND THE COMETS RELEASE "ROCK
AROUND THE CLOCK" . . . FIRST
ISSUE OF "SPORTS ILLUSTRATED"
IS PUBLISHED . . .

JULY 12

Welterweight Tony DeMarco,
hailing from Boston's North End,
scores a 10th-round triumph
over George Araujo in an
outdoor fight at Fenway

JULY 29

Led by the great Goose
Tatum, the Harlem Globetrotters
perform; it is the first basketball
game ever played at Fenway

1955

>>>>>>

. . . BILL RUSSELL AND THE
SAN FRANCISCO DONS WIN NCAA
TOURNAMENT . . . ROSA PARKS
REFUSES TO GIVE UP BUS SEAT IN
ALABAMA . . . DISNEYLAND OPENS . . .

APRIL 14 >

Ted Williams sits out
Opening Day at Fenway,
and the first month of the
season, because of a divorce
settlement with wife Doris.
When he returns in mid-May,
joining Boston's other big
bats—Jackie Jensen and Jimmy
Piersall—Williams hits a home
run in his first game back

ONE FOR THE BOOKS

Jimmy Piersall's mental breakdown while playing for the Red Sox brought shame and fame

FROM THE MOUND AT Fenway Park on June 11, 1952, St. Louis Browns pitcher Satchel Paige couldn't believe what he was seeing. Paige, having made the transformation from Negro leagues star to major league star, had just entered the game in relief. On third base, having hit a single earlier in the inning, was a young Red Sox outfielder named Jimmy Piersall. From third, Piersall began imitating Paige's uniquely long windup, then flapped his arms like a chicken and made oinking noises like a pig. After Piersall scored, Paige could still hear Piersall mocking him from the dugout. Unnerved, Paige would later give up a game-winning grand slam.

A month later, Piersall was in a mental hospital with "nervous exhaustion." This had not been an isolated incident. Piersall had engaged in a number of fights and verbal spats, both on and off the field, with opponents and with teammates. He was diagnosed with bipolar disorder and missed the remainder of the '52 season. He rejoined the Red Sox the next season and enjoyed a comeback year, even finishing ninth in the AL MVP voting. He would continue to play well for Boston, twice making the All-Star team, until he was traded to Cleveland after the '58

In the Fenway locker room in May of 1955, Piersall joined his collaborator, Al Hirshberg, to celebrate their new book.

season. (Piersall would finish his career with 104 homers and 591 RBIs.)

While he could never escape his past troubles—and would continue to have outbursts of bizarre behavior throughout his career—Piersall came to accept his condition. Many of his problems, he decided, came from his father, who put enormous pressure on him

when he was young to become a professional ballplayer. So thoroughly did Piersall acknowledge his embarrassments that he wrote an autobiography, titled *Fear Strikes Out*. The book was made into a movie in '57, using bits of real game footage from Fenway to enhance the film. The drama of Piersall's mental health ultimately overshadowed his talent as a ballplayer but secured his fame. As he wrote in the first line of a later book, "Probably the best thing that ever happened to me was going nuts."

MAY 6

The book *Fear Strikes Out*, by Boston centerfielder Jimmy Piersall, is released, chronicling his 1952 emotional collapse and recovery

MAY 27

Red Sox rookie first baseman Norm Zauchin hits three home runs and sets a Fenway Park record by driving in 10 runs

1956

〉〉〉〉〉〉

... ROCKY MARCIANO, THE BROCKTON BRAWLER, RETIRES WITH 49-0 RECORD ... "THE TEN COMMANDMENTS" OPENS IN THEATERS ... NATION'S INTERSTATE HIGHWAY SYSTEM IS BORN ...

‹ APRIL 17

On Opening Day, the Red
Sox beat Baltimore 8-1, pleasing not only a full house inside Fenway but also a happy horde of young fans gathered outside the bleachers

‹ JULY 14

Boston southpaw Mel
Parnell hurls a no-hitter against the Chicago White Sox, the first Red Sox pitcher to throw a no-hitter at Fenway since 1923

‹ AUGUST 7

After dropping a fly ball hit by
Mickey Mantle, Williams is booed by Fenway fans. After then snaring a Yogi Berra drive at the fence, he's cheered as he returns to the dugout. But Williams infamously spits toward fans and is later fined $5,000 by Boston G.M. Joe Cronin for "misconduct on the field"

^ AUGUST 17

Mike (Pinky) Higgins, here watching the Senators take batting practice, is the Boston manager after previously being a Red Sox third baseman. Though later the team's G.M., and always popular, his career of general mediocrity is reflected in his record as manager: 560–556

1957

〉〉〉〉〉〉

. . . OKLAHOMA SOONERS WIN STREAK ENDS AT 47 . . . JOHN F. KENNEDY WINS PULITZER PRIZE FOR "PROFILES IN COURAGE" . . . JOHN LENNON AND PAUL McCARTNEY MEET AT CHURCH DANCE . . .

^ MAY 26

The Massachusetts SPCA, responding to reports that Ted Williams had been shooting pigeons in leftfield, stakes out Fenway, attempting to nab him

‹ AUGUST 15

The movie version of *Fear Strikes Out* opens, with Anthony Perkins starring in the role of Jimmy Piersall. Stock footage of Fenway is used in the film, but scenes with Perkins shot elsewhere are discrepancies duly noted by Boston fans

1958

>>>>>>

*. . . BOSTON'S WEST END IS
DEMOLISHED IN URBAN RENEWAL
PROJECT . . . ELVIS PRESLEY ENTERS
U.S. ARMY . . . COLTS BEAT GIANTS
IN OVERTIME FOR NFL TITLE . . .*

^ JUNE 8

Red Sox rightfielder Jackie
Jensen hits two home runs,
including a 10th-inning game
winner to beat Chicago 6-5. He
is on his way to being named
AL MVP; for the season he hits
35 homers and has 122 RBIs

^ JUNE 23

TV luminary Ed Sullivan
appears at Fenway Park to
help host the annual Mayor's
Charity Field Day

‹ JULY 20

Jim Bunning, Detroit Tigers
pitcher (and future U.S.
Senator from Kentucky),
throws a no-hitter against the
Red Sox, winning 3-0

IN MR. YAWKEY'S YARD

During his four decades as owner of the Red Sox, including the often frustrating '50s, Tom Yawkey, more than anyone else, preserved the dignity and distinctiveness of Fenway

EVEN WITH AN OCEAN breeze blowing up the Charles River, Fenway Park seems to give off the faint, agreeable mustiness of a gentleman's club. Like so many of the best Boston institutions it is fronted with red brick. The solid oak door that leads from the street to the executive offices gleams with brass and varnish, and would do justice to a Beacon Hill town house. Set into the bricks not far from the door is one of those bronze plaques that decorate old Boston buildings, verifying them as The Real Thing. This particular plaque, bearing the sort of honorific prose ordinarily devoted to Tea Party revolutionaries, commemorates Edward Trowbridge Collins, perhaps the best of all second basemen and also the Red Sox general manager from 1933 to 1947.

Fenway Park sits in the Fens area of Back Bay, in what may fairly be termed the cultural preserve of Boston, a few blocks walking distance from the Museum of Fine Arts, Harvard Medical School and Symphony Hall, the redbrick home of the Boston Symphony Orchestra. Among such proper Bostonians the dapper little park does not seem out of place. Fenway, built in 1912, rebuilt in 1934, belongs to the era when a ballpark, in the manner of other civic buildings, took on the character of its community. Fenway Park *is* Boston, or what Boston used to be.

Inside, the park presents a first impression of spare, puritanical tidiness. The playing field is the rich green against which all baseball greens must be measured. There are no electronic waterfall-and-cartoon marvels that light up like a Christmas tree when a native son hits a home run. The very thought would make a Fenway fan shudder. When a Red Sox rally is on, the organ does not lead the charge. A Fenway fan would be insulted if it did. Fenway Park is emphatically not a fun emporium.

Yawkey, in his box with his wife Jean, guarded his privacy, often choosing to suffer the travails of his Red Sox alone.

It is a place for knowledgeable fans. In the self-assured Boston sense that Symphony Hall is the home for Good Music, Fenway Park is the home for Good Baseball.

The visitor who has been lost on Boston streets—those vestigial cowpaths perpetuated by Yankee surveyors—will laugh or cry or rage, depending on his temperament, when he recognizes the same random pattern at work in Fenway Park. The edge of the playing field is defined by 10 or 11 zigs and zags, according to how you count. The effect is of a jigsaw puzzle with at least one piece willfully fitted wrong. The most famous section of the puzzle is, of course, the leftfield wall, more or less affectionately known as the Green Monster. And across the way in rightfield, this innocent-looking stadium boasts one of the most intimidating sun fields in baseball. In Boston, so goes the

folklore, the sun rises in the east and sets in the eyes of the rightfielder. The first sunglasses ever used in baseball were purchased from Lloyds of Boston by Red Sox rightfielder Harry Hooper of the brilliant pre-World War I outfield of Hooper, Tris Speaker and Duffy Lewis.

If a ballpark can be said to have character, then the city of Boston, the zig-zags, the Monster and all the rest have given their stamp to Fenway Park. But nothing and nobody has put an imprint on this quaint, perfervid home for Boston baseball like Thomas Austin Yawkey. Fenway Park comes close to being a projection of his state of mind.

Yawkey bought the Red Sox in 1933 as a 30th birthday present to himself, four days after coming into nobody knows how many millions of dollars. Tom Yawkey is the sort of character who would have fascinated F. Scott Fitzgerald. He is the last of those enormously rich young men who bought themselves baseball teams as grown-ups' toys the way other young men today might buy a sailboat or a motorcycle. Something called Thomas Yawkey Enterprises exists in New York, representing the timber, mines and golden etceteras Yawkey's fortune is tied up in. Yawkey regularly graces those premises by his absence. Between October and April he retreats to his plantation on an island off South Carolina that constitutes his other toy: a 40,000-acre game preserve. Between May and October, Yawkey occupies a suite at the Ritz-Carlton and spends large parts of his days and nights at Fenway Park. Before night games Yawkey eats dinner (often a steak) in a paneled dining room–lounge off his office, surrounded by such memorabilia as the silvered bats of Ted Williams. The owner and his wife have adjacent his and her boxes on the skyview terrace. Nobody enters Tom Yawkey's box without invitation.

Friendly, even convivial as a younger man, Yawkey has grown more remote through the years. He dislikes being interviewed or photographed. He still pays the kind of salaries that brought down upon the Red Sox embarrassing epithets like the Millionaires and the Gold Sox long before the superaffluent athlete had arrived elsewhere. Yawkey will hero-worship baseball players till the day he dies. But things have changed. "Tom" to earlier generations of Red Sox players—to hunting pals like Lefty Grove and Mike Higgins—he is now "Mister Yawkey." The Red Sox press continues to be treated royally. The dining room at Fenway Park serves the writers in a style to which they ought not to become accustomed. But the days are past when Yawkey circulated freely among them, an old Yale man in his fraternity.

A visitor to Fenway Park on an off-day feels a little like a friend of the butler in a Jane Austen novel being shown about the master's house on the sly. Yawkey's office area is referred to by staff as "out-of-bounds." One almost tiptoes as one approaches the clubhouse. "Is he *there*?" The question goes out in a sort of chain whisper from one employee to another. Evidently the prospect of bursting in on Yawkey on the massage table rates with surprising Queen Victoria in her bath.

Yawkey seems to haunt Fenway Park like a castle ghost. When he walks the corridors and tunnels and climbs the angular stairs of Fenway this lank man with a squint and the creased leather face of a Brooks Brothers frontiersman, what does he see? Other ghosts, perhaps.

Look. In back of second base the handsome, dour Bobby Doerr—who maintains the posture of a career Army officer even when bending

> ❝ When he walks the corridors and tunnels and climbs the angular stairs, Yawkey seems to haunt Fenway Park like a castle ghost. ❞

over a ground ball—is stealing base hits off the grass. Joe Cronin, the "Boy Manager" for whom the Red Sox in 1934 paid an unprecedented top dollar of $250,000, is describing mincing little circles at shortstop, all worried jaw and hunched shoulders. Joe is trying to decide whether to yank Wes Ferrell, a big wavy-haired country boy who is scratching up furious clouds of dust around the rubber. Wes, in turn, is trying to decide whether to walk off the mound without permission or, on the contrary, to refuse to be relieved. (He may be the only pitcher to be fined for doing both.)

Meanwhile, in the rightfield bullpen built in 1940 to meet a Ted Williams home run halfway, Moe Berg, part-time catcher, part-time American spy—a Princeton graduate who could speak a dozen languages, including Japanese and Sanskrit—is delivering a lecture to the relief pitchers on the 19th-century Russian novel.

For the privilege of these sights, these memories, Yawkey has paid out a sum variously estimated between $10 million and $40 million. Where would Fenway Park be without him? The season's attendance in 1932, the year before Yawkey, was down to 182,150. Fenway Park might well have become just another Boston

public building on its way to being condemned, plastered with posters of other entertainments, as it was when its owner was the forgettable Harry Frazee, producer of *No, No, Nanette*. Yawkey has saved Boston baseball from that, not only by his money but by his pride.

Yawkey is the last of the dilettante sportsmen, the gentlemen owners, the George Apleys of baseball. What the name of Lowell is to the Boston Symphony and the name of Eliot is to Harvard, the name of Yawkey is to Boston baseball. He is not only an owner but a patron.

Yawkey has survived to live in a world where percentages refer to profits and write-offs as much as winning and losing. Yawkey wants to win at his games as only a man can want to win who has had everything else in life given to him. This genteel man dreams of seeing the banner of world champion fly over his genteel old park: one moment of glory before all things old-fashioned disappear.

POSTSCRIPT *Yawkey would keep watch over his Red Sox until the day he died, in July 1976, some nine months after the Sox had lost Game 7 of the '75 World Series. In his 43 years of ownership, he never got to celebrate a world championship.*

1959

›››››››

. . . CELTICS BEGIN STREAK OF EIGHT STRAIGHT NBA TITLES . . . REBEL LEADER FIDEL CASTRO TAKES CONTROL OF CUBA . . . "BEN-HUR" OPENS, GOES ON TO WIN 11 OSCARS . . .

‹ **AUGUST 4**

Pumpsie Green, the first African-American to play for the Red Sox, makes his Fenway debut at second base and hits a triple; Boston is the last team in the major leagues to integrate its roster

‹ **AUGUST 23**

Jazz great Duke Ellington plays Fenway, along with Dinah Washington, as part of the Boston Jazz Festival

1960
TO
1969

Williams says goodbye with a home run ~ Tony C. gets decked ~ The Patriots make Fenway home ~ The wait is over: The Red Sox win the pennant

October 5, 1967
Carl Yastrzemski, concluding his Triple Crown season, leads the Red Sox against the Cardinals in the World Series.
Photograph by NEIL LEIFER

1960

>>>>>

. . . BOSTON PATRIOTS BEGIN
PLAY AT BU'S NICKERSON FIELD
. . . JOHN F. KENNEDY IS ELECTED
PRESIDENT, DEFEATS RICHARD
NIXON . . . THE QUARRYMEN
BECOME THE BEATLES . . .

AUGUST 30

Boston second baseman Pete
Runnels, in a doubleheader with
the Tigers, has nine hits to tie
a major league record

SEPTEMBER 28

In the last at bat of his
career, Williams strokes a
home run, his 521st. At home
plate, Williams shakes the
hand of Jim Pagliaroni, then
disappears into the dugout.
The Fenway crowd roars,
beseeching him to emerge and
tip his cap. He does not

1961

>>>>>

. . . ROGER MARIS BREAKS
BABE RUTH'S HOME RUN RECORD
WITH 61 . . . ALAN SHEPARD
OF DERRY, N.H., IS THE FIRST
AMERICAN IN SPACE . . . SINGER
MERV GRIFFIN RELEASES SINGLE
"BANNED IN BOSTON" . . .

HERB SCHARFMAN: AP (OPPOSITE)

When the hated and dominant Yankees arrive in town, leading the Red Sox by 31½ games in the standings, the crowd outside Fenway mobs the Yankee bus—but shows more curiosity than animosity

APRIL 25 >

Gene Conley, who previously played basketball for the Boston Celtics, makes his Red Sox pitching debut at Fenway. He already owns the distinction of being the only player to win pro championships in two major sports (with the Celtics and Milwaukee Braves)

^
JUNE 20

Cab Calloway, bandleader and scat singer, brings his act to Fenway for the Mayor's Charity Field Day event

< JULY 31

Williams, recently retired, throws out the first ball at the All-Star Game at Fenway. Play is halted in the ninth inning by torrential rain with the score 1-1, causing the first tie in All-Star Game history

1962

>>>>>>

...WILT CHAMBERLAIN SCORES
100 POINTS FOR PHILADELPHIA
...BOSTON STRANGLER
MURDERS BEGIN... ANDY
WARHOL UNVEILS CAMPBELL'S
SOUP CANS EXHIBIT...

JUNE 19

Starlet Zsa-Zsa Gabor
appears at Fenway for the
Mayor's Charity Field Day, along
with singer Dennis Day

< **JUNE 26**

Boston's Earl Wilson no-hits
the Los Angeles Angels in a
2-0 win, becoming the first
African-American to throw
a no-hitter in the American
League. Wilson also puts up
the only run he'll need with
a third-inning home run off
Angels starter Bo Belinsky

1963

>>>>>>

...JFK IS ASSASSINATED IN
DALLAS... PRO FOOTBALL HALL
OF FAME OPENS IN CANTON,
OHIO... FCC AUTHORIZES USE OF
TELEVISION REMOTE CONTROL...

^
APRIL 9
_____

A new scoreboard is erected
behind Fenway's rightfield
bleachers and gets the
finishing touches

‹ **MAY 12**
_____

On Cape Cod Day, Senator Ted
Kennedy throws out the first ball to
Sox catcher Russ Nixon, who also
catches the irony of the connection
to the 1960 Presidential election

AUGUST 19 ›
_____

Slugger Dick Stuart hits an
inside-the-park home run when the
ball bounces crazily off Fenway's
leftfield ladder, then off Cleveland
centerfielder Vic Davalillo's head

^
OCTOBER 11
_____

Fenway's field is readied for
a football game between the
AFL's Boston Patriots and
Oakland Raiders, in the first of
six seasons that the Patriots
make Fenway their home

A HIDDEN GEM

Pitcher Dave Morehead made Fenway history, but there are very few who can say they witnessed it

I T WAS A THURSDAY AFTERNOON game in mid-September of 1965 against the Cleveland Indians, and with the Red Sox long out of contention and staggering towards a 100-loss season, it was not exactly a hot ticket. Just 1,247 fans showed up at Fenway as 22-year-old Red Sox righty Dave Morehead took the mound. Who knows how many fans were still there nine innings later when Morehead finished off his no-hitter, the 14th in Red Sox history. It was a brilliant performance, with Morehead walking just one batter and beating the Indians 2–0, in exactly two hours.

It was a rare chance for the Red Sox to celebrate, yet even that was a muted affair; after the game, Boston general manager Pinky Higgins was fired.

The game was not only the highlight of Boston's dreary season, but of Morehead's time in the major leagues. The San Diego native's career had once looked bright. He'd won 28 games his first three seasons, but in '65 would wind up losing 18 games, more than any other AL pitcher, and would never again win more than five games in a season. By 1971 he was out of baseball. Still, his no-hitter had lasting resonance—it would be 37 years until it happened at Fenway again.

FRANK CURTIN/AP; AP (OPPOSITE)

1964

>>>>>>

...PRUDENTIAL TOWER IS COMPLETED IN BOSTON... DR. MARTIN LUTHER KING IS YOUNGEST NOBEL PEACE PRIZE WINNER... RICHARD PETTY WINS FIRST OF RECORD SEVEN DAYTONA 500S...

SEPTEMBER 24

Republican presidential candidate Barry Goldwater speaks to a Fenway crowd of 20,000. Five weeks later he will lose the election in a landslide to Lyndon Johnson

DECEMBER 20

In a battle for the AFL East crown, Buffalo quarterback (and future Republican congressman) Jack Kemp leads the Bills to a 24-14 win over the Patriots. Kemp passes for one TD and runs for two more

1965

>>>>>>

...JACK NICKLAUS SHOOTS RECORD 271 TO WIN MASTERS ...FIRST U.S. COMBAT TROOPS ARRIVE IN VIETNAM... BOSTON SEGMENT OF MASSACHUSETTS TURNPIKE OPENS...

MAY 16

Cities Service changes its corporate name to Citgo. By midsummer a sign will stand over Kenmore Square bearing the new logo

MAY 30 ›

Empty seats abound as few fans show up to see the woeful Red Sox play the Kansas City A's; the Sox will lose 100 games in '65. (The record for smallest crowd in Fenway Park history had been set on Oct. 1 the previous fall: 306 fans saw the Sox beat the Indians)

SEPTEMBER 16

Boston's Dave Morehead throws a no-hitter, beating the Cleveland Indians. Alas, his feat is witnessed by mostly empty Fenway seats

NOVEMBER 14

Girls from Radcliffe College are cheerleaders at Fenway for the Boston Patriots, but fail to lift the Pats, who lose 30-20 to the New York Jets

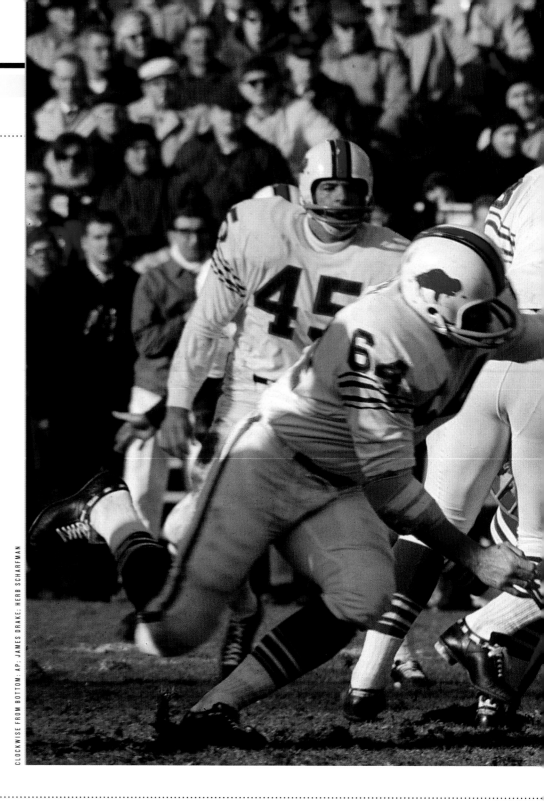

CLOCKWISE FROM BOTTOM: AP; JAMES DRAKE; HERB SCHARFMAN

1966

>>>>>>

...MAO TSE-TUNG BEGINS
CULTURAL REVOLUTION...BOBBY
ORR, AGE 18, JOINS BOSTON
BRUINS...TEXAS WESTERN
BEATS KENTUCKY IN NCAA
BASKETBALL FINAL...

‹ JULY 21

At age 21, Tony Conigliaro, already the reigning AL home run champ (32 in '65), takes tips from club VP Ted Williams in the Red Sox locker room

JULY 24 ›

Four year-old Mike Yastrzemski, with a little help from dad Carl (8), fires his fastball in the annual Red Sox father-son game

A RUN TO THE TOP

In an excerpt from SI in December of '66, writer Edwin Shrake hails the fullback of the surprising Pats

BY BEATING BUFFALO ON Sunday the amazing Boston Patriots have taken the lead in the American Football League's Eastern Division. The very fact that Boston is up there at all is cause for astonishment. It should be enough to make Mike Holovak the AFL's Coach of the Year and fullback Jim Nance—who got the Patriots moving on offense with a brilliant, battering 65-yard touchdown run—the league's most valuable player. It ought to win a year's supply of cigars for quarterback Babe Parilli.

In the first quarter on a bright, cold day, on third-and-two when everybody in the sellout crowd of 39,350 at Fenway Park knew it would be Nance carrying the ball, the big fullback crashed into an excellent Buffalo defensive line that was massed against him. He broke two tackles, stumbled but regained his balance and ran for his touchdown.

This year's AFL championship game will be played in the East, where frozen ground might give Nance an edge. Nance, however, is thinking beyond that. "I want to play those NFL guys," he says. "I'm sick of hearing people say we're not good enough to play in that league."

‹ JULY 29

On Nuns' Day at Fenway, a group of sisters are steadfast as the Red Sox take a 2-0 lead over Kansas City; but the heavens don't cooperate, and the game is called in the third inning on account of rain

‹ DECEMBER 4

Patriots fullback Jim Nance makes the cover of SPORTS ILLUSTRATED after the Pats beat the Buffalo Bills 14-3. Boston QB Babe Parilli, who ran for a score, savors a victory cigar

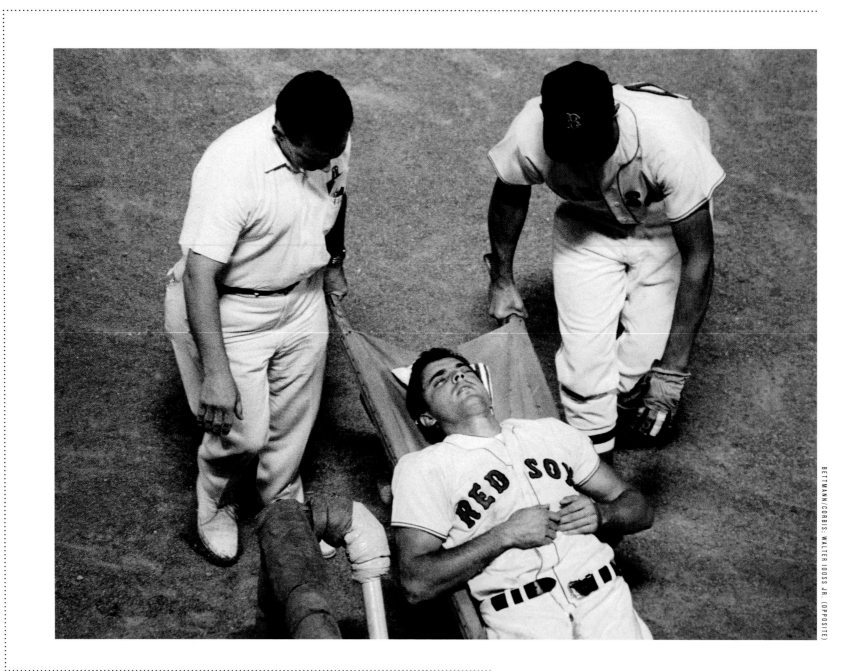

BETTMANN/CORBIS; WALTER IOOSS JR. (OPPOSITE)

1967

>>>>>

...PACKERS DEFEAT CHIEFS IN
SUPER BOWL I...APOLLO I FIRE
KILLS THREE ASTRONAUTS...
CELTICS STUN BOSTON BY NOT
WINNING NBA TITLE—FALLING
TO WILT CHAMBERLAIN AND
PHILADELPHIA IN EAST FINALS—
CELTS' ONLY NONCHAMPIONSHIP
SEASON OF THE DECADE...

‹ AUGUST 18

In a frightening
episode, Tony Conigliaro
is hit in the face by a pitch
from the Angels' Jack
Hamilton. Carried from
the field under the eye
of Red Sox trainer Buddy
LeRoux, Conigliaro has a
fractured left cheek and
damaged left eye

‹ OCTOBER 1 ›

After the Red Sox beat the
Twins 5-3 to win the AL
pennant, their first in 21 years,
winning pitcher Jim Lonborg
gets a police escort from
the field and Yastrzemski
celebrates in the shower

OCTOBER 1

Yastrzemski wins the Triple
Crown after wielding this bat
for seven hits in his last eight
Fenway at bats. He is baseball's
last Triple Crown winner

OCTOBER 2

The Fenway faithful wait
outside the park to buy tickets
to the World Series—playing
chess to pass the time

OCTOBER 4

In Game 1 of the World Series, Rico
Petrocelli tags the Cardinals' Lou
Brock on a steal of second, but Brock
is called safe. The Sox fall to Bob
Gibson and the Cards, 2–1

FROM LEFT: BETTMANN/CORBIS; TONY TRIOLO; WALTER IOOSS JR.

OCTOBER 5

Jim Lonborg's masterly one-hitter in Game 2 of the Series, a 5–0 Boston win, goes down as a Fenway classic

OCTOBER 7 ›

The Red Sox lose Game 7, at home, 7–2, again to the great Gibson; in the Fenway locker room afterward, Boston manager Dick Williams gives reporters his postmortem

1968

››››››

. . . *MARTIN LUTHER KING AND ROBERT KENNEDY ARE ASSASSINATED; AFTER MLK SHOOTING, SINGER JAMES BROWN HELPS QUELL BOSTON UNREST . . . TOMMIE SMITH AND JOHN CARLOS GIVE BLACK POWER SALUTE AT '68 OLYMPICS IN MEXICO CITY . . . "60 MINUTES" DEBUTS ON CBS . . .*

JULY 8

Pelé draws over 18,000 fans to watch his Santos club beat the Boston Beacons. It will be 42 years before soccer returns to Fenway

Excerpted from SPORTS ILLUSTRATED 4.7.69

BY MARK MULVOY

THE RETURN OF TONY C

Nearly 20 months after being hit by a pitch and badly hurt at Fenway, Tony Conigliaro was back at the plate, defying the doctors and proving that he was a hitter again

FROM THE START OF 1969 spring training it was almost certain that a Conigliaro would be playing rightfield for the Boston Red Sox when the first pitch was delivered in the home opener at Fenway Park. Maybe it would be Tony, age 24, providing he could really see a baseball with both eyes again, something the top specialists in the country once said was impossible. Or it might be Tony's brother Billy, 21, young and inexperienced, perhaps, but possessing enough ability and aggressiveness to play in the majors right now.

As of last week, there was no longer any doubt about which Conigliaro will start in rightfield. It will be Tony—Tony C—back again in his old position and batting fifth in the Red Sox lineup. Brother Billy will be sitting on the Boston bench.

Tony did not win the rightfield job; he simply reclaimed it. Certainly Billy did not lose it. Indeed, with only one week of the exhibition schedule left, he was outhitting his older brother by more than 50 points. Billy easily was the best rookie in the Red Sox camp, just like Tony was their best rookie in 1964.

However, Billy's accomplishments this spring, impressive as they were, were not nearly as dramatic as his brother's. Doctors say it is a medical miracle that Tony can see the white baseball with the red stitches when it is pitched to him at varying speeds and angles from a distance of 60 feet six inches. And Tony always has been able to hit a baseball when he has seen it—or when it has not hit him.

Before his 23rd birthday Conigliaro had hit 104 home runs in the major leagues, more than any player in history at a comparative age. During his first four seasons, though, he was injured seriously five times, when wild pitches fractured his left hand, right wrist, right arm, shoulder blade and left cheekbone.

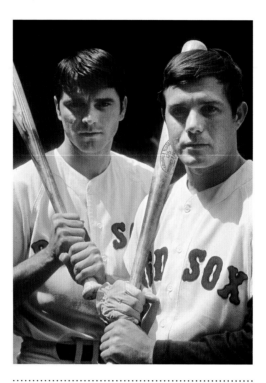

The brothers Conigliaro, Tony (left) and Billy, both made it to Fenway, both of them glad to be Red Sox.

The cheekbone was fractured the night of Aug. 18, 1967, in Fenway, in the fourth inning of a game against the California Angels. Tony was anticipating a pitch away from the plate. The pitcher, Jack Hamilton, threw inside instead, and Conigliaro could not get out of the way. The ball smashed against the left side of his face, just below his temple and parallel to his eye. Tony was rushed to the hospital. "I knew it was bad," he said. "I dozed off for 20 minutes and when I woke up there was blood all over the sheets."

Conigliaro was confident that the cheekbone eventually would heal—after all, the other bones all had healed properly. He was more concerned about his eyes. For almost two days he could not see anything. Then the right eye cleared completely. But, when he left the hospital a week later, the left eye still was virtually useless.

Tony did not play again in 1967. Last spring he reported to the Red Sox '68 training camp. He thought his left eye was better, but it was immediately obvious that he was wrong, that he couldn't see the ball. He was falling away from the plate almost before the pitcher released the ball. In the old days Tony Conigliaro never fell back. He propped himself over the plate, bat cocked vertically and dared the pitcher to throw the ball past him.

When Tony did swing at pitches last spring, he missed them badly. He struck out four times in one game against the Yankees. Three days later he struck out three more times against the Senators. Afterward he went into the Red Sox clubhouse, locked the door behind him and almost destroyed the room. For 10 minutes he threw chairs and bats and balls and gloves to relieve his frustration. That night, he returned to Boston to see the eye doctors once more.

A team of specialists at the Retina Foundation in Boston examined Tony's left eye. They discovered a hole in his macula, the section of the retina containing the nerve fibers and specialized rods and cones that provide sharp vision. Tests showed that Conigliaro had almost no depth perception and that the sight in his left eye, once 20/15, was 20/300. It was then the doctors told Tony that he never would be able to see well enough out of that left eye to hit a baseball again.

Tony and his father, Sal, drove home to Swampscott, a North Shore suburb of Boston. It was a quiet ride. When they got home, Sal told Mrs. Conigliaro that Tony's career was finished. Tony went to his bedroom and locked himself there for days, emerging only to eat. "I couldn't blame the kid," Sal Conigliaro said. "Then I came home from work one day and found my lawn all dug up. Tony had made a pitcher's mound and he had measured off the distance to the plate. He was out there pitching to his brother Richie."

Tom Yawkey, the Red Sox owner, had told Tony that he never would have to worry about his future, that there would always be a job for him with the Red Sox. There were several other careers open to Conigliaro. He already was a professional singer whose records had sold well. And a Boston television station offered to send him to TV school. But now Tony wanted to be a major league pitcher.

Last winter he went to Florida to pitch for the Red Sox team in the instructional league. Once there, he got an itch to step back into the batting cage. Tony hit the ball hard. He could see the ball again, he claimed, almost the way he used to see it before he was beaned that August night.

Heartened, he returned to Boston for another examination at the Retina Foundation. The same doctors who explained the macula hole to Tony only seven months earlier were now dumbfounded. Somehow, the hole had filled with pigment. "It was a miraculous thing," one specialist told the Red Sox' doctor. "Somebody must have said a novena for that kid."

Tests disclosed that Tony had regained the depth perception in his left eye and that the sight in the eye had improved to 20/20.

And so, Conigliaro began his comeback at camp in Winter Haven, Fla. "He didn't look good in early batting practices," said Jerry Stephenson, a Red Sox pitcher. "Everyone hits then, but Tony was missing the ball." Conigliaro had an explanation. "I could see the ball all right," he said. "I could pick up the spin. But I hadn't played in more than a year and a half

and I was trying to get comfortable." Although most people around Winter Haven doubted Tony's explanation and believed he still could not see, Carl Yastrzemski decided right away that Tony, in fact, was all right. "Good hitters can start themselves into the pitch, look at the ball and then check themselves if they see the ball is going to be outside the strike zone," Yaz said. "Tony always used to do that. Last year he swung at everything. He couldn't see the ball well enough to check his swing. He missed all the time. I looked at him in batting practice this spring and noticed he could check himself again. And that told me that he can see."

In his third game of the spring Tony was knocked down by a rookie pitcher for Minnesota. While Twins manager Billy Martin rushed to the mound to calm the rookie, Conigliaro bounced up and dusted himself off. The pitch had been close, but he was unperturbed.

GRADUALLY, TONY BEGAN to hit the ball solidly. He was moving closer to the plate every time at bat. He was using a bat 1½ inches longer than the one he used before the beaning, and he was not bailing out. His left foot was aimed to the right of first base—not the third base dugout. But it was

not until last week that Tony really began to hit like the old—or the young—Conigliaro. Against the Reds he singled sharply into centerfield in the first inning. "I was hitting the ball square, and that's all I really wanted," he said.

Until then Tony had not hit any home runs. But in the third inning, facing Mel Queen, Tony connected with a fastball. The ball disappeared over the leftfield fence and landed about 425 feet from home plate. When he returned to the dugout, his teammates swarmed around him.

There now was no longer any doubt that Tony Conigliaro could see the baseball. And there was no doubt that when the Red Sox got home, it would be Tony C standing again in rightfield at Fenway Park.

POSTSCRIPT *In the '69 season, Conigliaro would hit .255 with 20 home runs; in 1970 he was even better: .266 with 36 home runs. But following the '70 season, he was traded to the Angels, leaving a nasty feud in his wake when his brother Billy accused Carl Yastrzemski of helping to orchestrate the trade. As an Angel he played only one ineffective and injury-riddled season. And his vision began to fail again. In 1975 he attempted another comeback with the Red Sox, but was forced to retire because of permanently damaged eyesight.*

"It was a miraculous thing," one specialist told the Red Sox. "Somebody must have said a novena for that kid."

‹ AUGUST 16

Sox outfielder and man-about-town Ken (Hawk) Harrelson, posed for Sports Illustrated at Fenway; the '68 season would be his career-best as he finished third in the AL MVP voting

1969

›››››
. . . WOODSTOCK MUSIC FESTIVAL IS HELD IN BETHEL, N.Y. . . . NEIL ARMSTRONG IS FIRST TO WALK ON THE MOON . . . JOE NAMATH GUARANTEES VICTORY IN SUPER BOWL III AND DELIVERS . . .

JUNE 28

Bruno Sammartino beats the reviled "Killer" Kowalski in a no-holds-barred wrestling match before 17,000 at Fenway, the grapplers squaring off without a referee. *The Boston Globe* covers the event with an article by young staff writer Peter Gammons

SEPTEMBER 16

Neil Diamond's 45 single *Sweet Caroline* is released. The song will later become an eighth-inning tradition, played at every game at Fenway beginning in 2002. Diamond would sing the song at Fenway in a 2008 concert

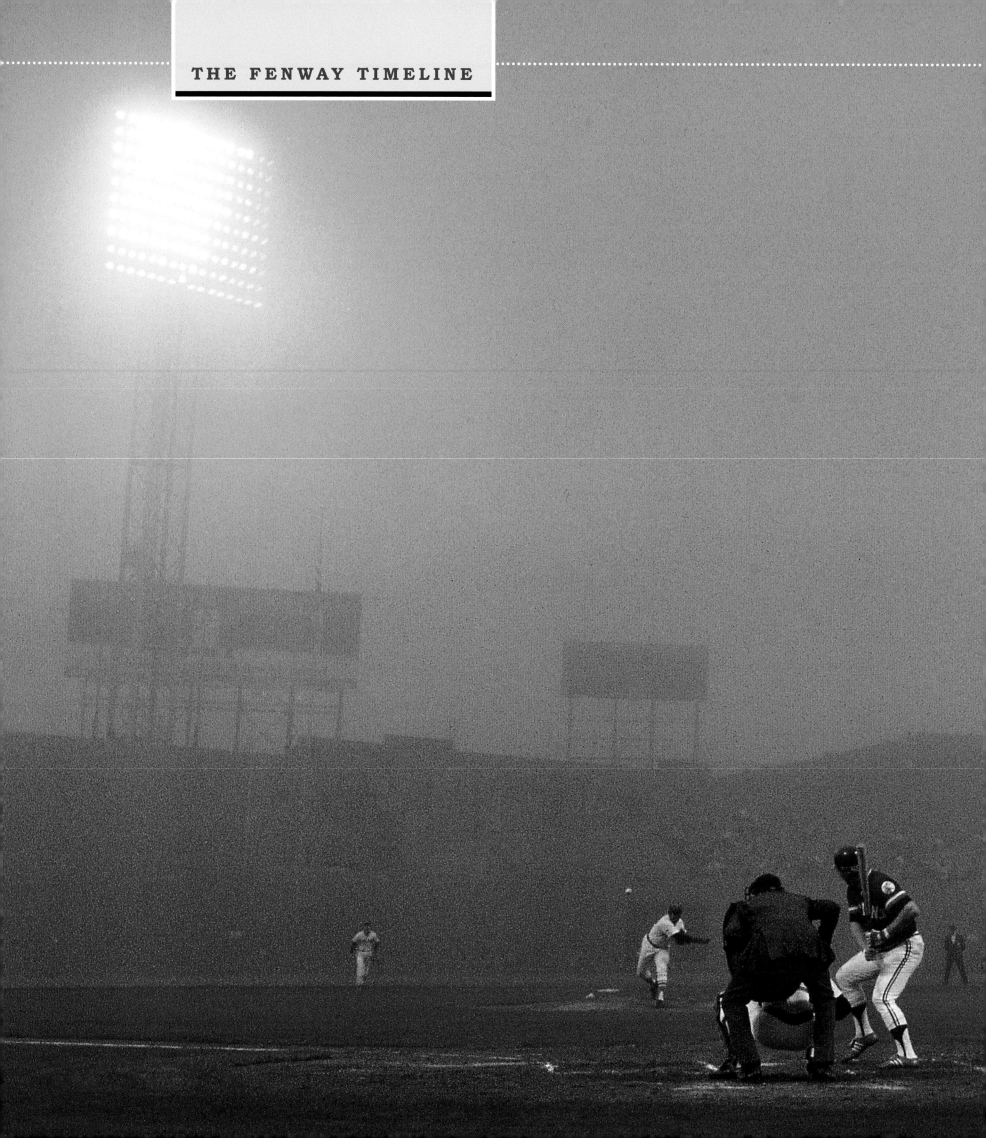

1970
TO
1979

A thrilling World Series ends in heartbreak ~ Carlton Fisk is a hero, Bucky Dent is a villain ~ Farewell to Fenway's father figure ~ Yaz makes his mark—twice

September 26, 1975
In the deepening Fenway mist late on a fall afternoon, Luis Tiant baffles the Cleveland Indians with a four-hit, 4–0 shutout.
Photograph by HEINZ KLUETMEIER

1970

›››››

. . .BOBBY ORR GOAL IN GAME 4 AGAINST ST. LOUIS CAPS BRUINS' FIRST STANLEY CUP SINCE 1941 . . . U.S. VOTING AGE IS LOWERED TO 18 . . . THE BEATLES DISBAND . . .

APRIL 14 ›

For the season opener at Fenway, the centerfield flagpole, which has been in the field of play since '34, is now enclosed by a fence extension

^
MAY 31

In a 40-hit slugfest, the Red Sox fall to the White Sox 22-13. But it's a beautiful afternoon at Fenway

1971

›››››

. . . IN FIRST WORLD SERIES NIGHT GAME, PIRATES BEAT THE ORIOLES . . . "NEW YORK TIMES" PUBLISHES THE PENTAGON PAPERS . . . WALT DISNEY WORLD OPENS IN ORLANDO . . .

JULY 15 ›

The Sox and Twins play one of the longest scoreless ties in Fenway history until Rico Petrocell hits a three-run homer in the bottom of the 13th to win it for Boston

DICK RAPHAEL

1972

>>>>>>

. . .RICHARD NIXON IMPLICATED IN
WATERGATE SCANDAL . . . BRUINS
WIN STANLEY CUP FOR SECOND
TIME IN THREE YEARS . . . COPPOLA
FILM "THE GODFATHER"
IS RELEASED . . .

SEPTEMBER 15

For the first time, the Red Sox allow
women reporters on to the field at
Fenway to talk to players; Madeline Blais
of *The Boston Globe* has questions for
Sox outfielder Reggie Smith

‹ SEPTEMBER 26

Boston pitcher Marty Pattin
hits a home run against
the Brewers. The DH rule is
adopted the following year;
no Red Sox pitcher has
homered at Fenway since

137

BEST BRAWL OF ALL

Two catchers collided and became the faces of a rivalry

IT WAS THE THIRD IN A FOUR-game series at Fenway between the Red Sox and Yankees, an afternoon affair on Aug. 1. With the score tied 2–2 in the top of the ninth, New York catcher Thurman Munson stood on third base with one out. With Gene Michael at the plate, a suicide squeeze was called. As Munson broke for home, Michael missed the bunt, leaving Boston catcher Carlton Fisk waiting at the plate; Munson lowered his shoulder and barreled into him with everything he could muster. Fisk held on to the ball for the out, but Munson lay atop him until Fisk wrestled him off. Fists flew, the benches emptied.

It remains a matter of argument as to who won the fight; both catchers scored with a number of good punches. It's an accepted matter of fact, though, that their brawl recharged a semidormant rivalry and would forever connect Fisk and Munson as the emblems of the teams' mutual disdain. Both men tried to play down any personal animosity, but there was plenty of evidence that Fisk and Munson just didn't like each other. They would ultimately each gain a triumph over the other. Munson would win two world championship rings, Fisk would never win one. Fisk would make the Hall of Fame; Munson would not.

1973

›››››››

...IN "ROE V. WADE," U.S. SUPREME COURT LIFTS BAN ON ABORTION...SECRETARIAT IS FIRST TRIPLE CROWN WINNER IN 25 YEARS...FIRST HANDHELD CELLULAR PHONE CALL IS MADE...

‹ **JANUARY 18**

Orlando Cepeda, 35, signs with the Sox, the first signing of a DH; he poses at Fenway with G.M. Dick O'Connell (far left) and VP Haywood Sullivan

^ **AUGUST 1**

Carlton Fisk and Yankee catcher Thurman Munson brawl after Munson bowls over Fisk in a collision at the plate

^ **JULY 28**

Stevie Wonder, among others, plays the Newport–New England Jazz Festival at Fenway. Because violence breaks out in various sections of the park, it will be the last concert in Fenway until 2003

1974

⟩⟩⟩⟩⟩⟩

...HANK AARON HITS NUMBER
715, PASSING BABE RUTH
TO BECOME HOME RUN KING
...GERALD FORD BECOMES
PRESIDENT AFTER NIXON RESIGNS
...BUSING ORDERED IN BOSTON
TO INTEGRATE PUBLIC SCHOOLS...

APRIL 30

After getting beaned by the Angels'
Nolan Ryan (below), Sox second baseman
Doug Griffin is sidelined for two months.
Griffin, ironically, had arrived via a trade
with the Angels for Tony Conigliaro

1975

⟩⟩⟩⟩⟩⟩

..."SATURDAY NIGHT
LIVE" PREMIERES ON NBC...
MUHAMMAD ALI DEFEATS JOE
FRAZIER IN "THRILLA IN MANILA"
...COMMUNIST TROOPS TAKE
SAIGON, ENDING VIETNAM WAR...

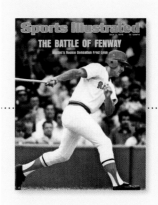

OCTOBER 10

Cincinnati's Pete Rose takes
in the Red Sox' workout at
Fenway the day before the
opener of the World Series

⟨ **JULY 7**

Outfielder Fred Lynn, the
Red Sox' rookie sensation
who's batting .339, makes the
cover of SPORTS ILLUSTRATED

139

‹ OCTOBER 11

In Game 1 of the '75
Series, Luis Tiant shows
his trademark back-to-the-
plate form to batter Pete
Rose. Afterward, El Tiante,
of Havana, celebrates his
6-0 shutout by lighting
up his trademark Cuban
victory cigar

‹ OCTOBER 12

Yaz greets Henry and Nancy
Kissinger prior to Game 2, as
commissioner Bowie Kuhn
looks on from behind

OCTOBER 12 ›

The bullpen cart returns after
taking Sox reliever Dick Drago to the
mound in the ninth; alas, he promptly
surrenders two runs in a 3-2 loss

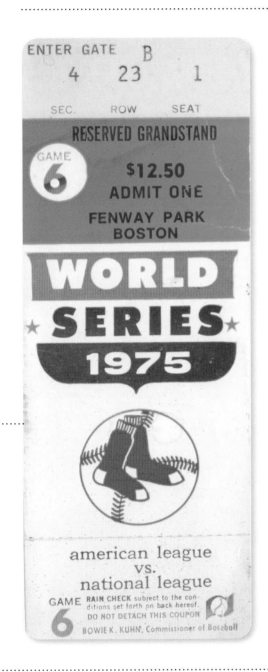

ENTER GATE B
4 23 1

SEC. ROW SEAT

RESERVED GRANDSTAND

GAME 6

$12.50

ADMIT ONE

FENWAY PARK
BOSTON

WORLD SERIES 1975

american league
vs.
national league

GAME 6 RAIN CHECK subject to the conditions set forth on back hereof. DO NOT DETACH THIS COUPON
BOWIE K. KUHN, Commissioner of Baseball

OCTOBER 19 ›

Game 6 is postponed three consecutive days by rain, but when finally played, it's worth the wait—a baseball classic

OCTOBER 21

Tickets for the Series range in price from $4 for bleacher seats to $20 for the best box seats. But *The Boston Globe* reports tickets being sold by scalpers for a shocking $100

OCTOBER 21 ›

Fred Lynn goes down after crashing into the wall in Game 6. For the following season, protective padding will be installed

‹ OCTOBER 21

Carlton Fisk scores the Game 6 game-winner after famously waving his 12th-inning home run to stay fair, perhaps the most treasured homer in Fenway Park history

141

OCTOBER 22

In the wake of another crushing Game 7 loss, this time 4-3 to the Reds, stunned Boston fans wander the field at Fenway

1976

⟩⟩⟩⟩⟩⟩

...SHIPS PARADE IN BOSTON HARBOR TO CELEBRATE U.S. BICENTENNIAL... BRUCE JENNER WINS THE DECATHLON AT THE MONTREAL OLYMPICS... SYLVESTER STALLONE'S "ROCKY" FILLS THEATERS...

MARCH 12 ⟩

The old ballpark gets a new look as an electronic scoreboard is installed and tested in centerfield

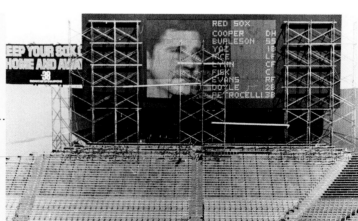

NEIL LEIFER; JOHN IACONO (OPPOSITE)

< JUNE 15

A's owner Charlie Finley sells Rollie
Fingers (above) and Joe Rudi to the
Red Sox for $1 million each in a fire
sale of his unsigned players. Three
days later commissioner Bowie Kuhn
overturns the transaction

^ JULY 9

Red Sox owner Tom Yawkey
dies at the age of 73. Yawkey,
a devoted steward of Fenway,
owned the team for 43 years,
the longest tenure by an
owner in baseball history

< JULY 20

Don Zimmer is named
Red Sox manager after
the firing of Darrell
Johnson. Zim will serve
for five seasons and
put together a record
of 411-304

1977

›››››

. . . *TAMPA BAY BUCS LOSE 26 STRAIGHT NFL GAMES . . . ATARI VCS GAME CONSOLE IS RELEASED . . . JAY LENO, FROM ANDOVER, MASS., MAKES FIRST "TONIGHT SHOW" GUEST APPEARANCE . . .*

‹ **JUNE 19**

Red Sox first baseman George (Boomer) Scott becomes the only player to hit home runs in games in five consecutive days at Fenway

˄ **SEPTEMBER 19**

Carlton Fisk and Butch Hobson dive for a foul off the bat of the Yankees' Roy White. Somehow Fisk catches the ball

‹ **JULY 4**

Giving the fans their holiday fireworks, Bernie Carbo is one of six Red Sox to homer, as Boston hits a total of eight home runs, a new team record for a single game

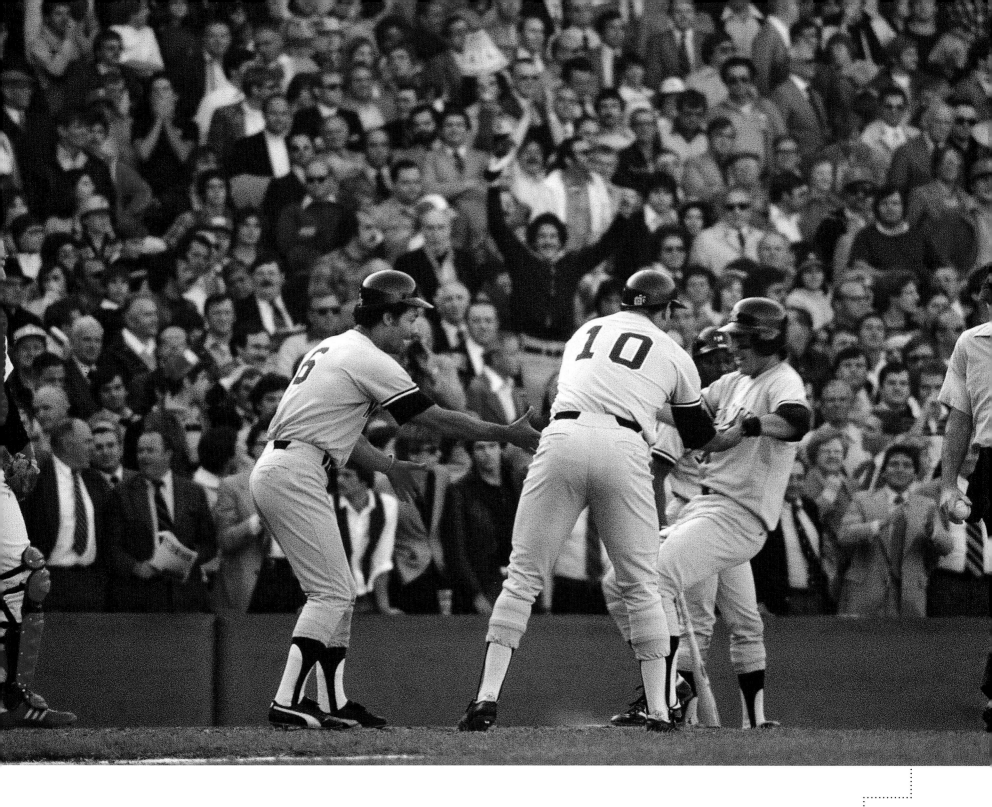

TONIGHT'S ATTENDANCE
20 362
SEASON TOTAL
2 004 649

1ST TIME THE RED SOX
HAVE REACHED
THE 2 MILLION MARK

SEPTEMBER 28

For the first time in the club's history, the Red Sox break through the two million mark in home attendance

1978

〉〉〉〉〉〉

. . . B.U. BEATS B.C. FOR NCAA ICE HOCKEY TITLE . . . FORD RECALLS THE PINTO DUE TO GAS TANK EXPLOSIONS . . . BLIZZARD DUMPS 27 INCHES OF SNOW ON BOSTON . . .

JULY 16 〉

Bill (Spaceman) Lee goes for laughs on the Fenway mound but gets serious about his clubhouse meditation

OCTOBER 2

Bucky Dent scores after his shocking three-run shot, leading to a bitter season-ending, 5–4 loss to the Yankees in the one-game playoff. Fenway fans will never forgive or forget

145

AP; MANNY MILLAN (OPPOSITE)

1979

〉〉〉〉〉〉

. . . LARRY BIRD AND INDIANA STATE FALL TO MICHIGAN STATE IN NCAA TITLE GAME . . . EGYPT AND ISRAEL SIGN CAMP DAVID PEACE TREATY. . . AMERICAN AIRLINES FLIGHT 191 CRASHES IN CHICAGO, U.S.'S DEADLIEST AVIATION ACCIDENT . . .

〈 **JANUARY 8**

Jim Rice, with G.M. Haywood Sullivan, signs a seven-year, $5.4 million contract, the largest yet for a Red Sox player

^
MARCH 4

Red Sox VP Buddy LeRoux, seeking to expand Fenway, suggests he will move the team to suburban Wilmington if not appeased by mayor Kevin White

^
JULY 24

Yastrzemski hits his 400th home run, off the A's Mike Morgan, nearly a month after hitting number 399, and is greeted at the plate by teammate Bob Watson and a new friend

Excerpted from **SPORTS ILLUSTRATED 9.24.79**

BY PETER GAMMONS

3,000 FINALLY

After being able to do pretty much whatever he wanted in the game of baseball during his brilliant career, Carl Yastrzemski found it suddenly surprisingly hard to get his historic hit

WHEN IT CAME, IT came simply and—considering the occasion—undramatically, a routine ground ball just past the reach of Yankee second baseman Willie Randolph with two outs and no one on in the ninth inning of a 9–2 game at Fenway Park. But the point was that it had come, at last, and as Carl Yastrzemski rounded first base shortly after 9:39 p.m. on Wednesday, Sept. 12, the celebration began. Horns blared, streamers sailed from the Fenway bleachers. Yaz had his 3,000th hit, becoming the 15th player to get that many in the majors and the first American Leaguer to have 3,000 hits and 400 home runs.

As the game was stopped and teammates, Yankees, family, fans, photographers, owners, politicians, publicity hounds and security guards engulfed Yastrzemski, his face showed the strain of the previous few days. "I just wish it were over," he had said repeatedly to the horde of newsmen who had followed him. Now it was.

"I know one thing," Yaz said to the giddy crowd of 34,336 when he stepped to a microphone that had been brought to the first base coach's box, "this one was the hardest of the 3,000." He laughed and continued, "I took so long to do it because I've enjoyed all those standing ovations you've given me the last three days." Then, seriously, "I've faced all kinds of pressure situations before, but none of them ever bothered me. This did. I was almost embarrassed I hadn't gotten it the last couple of days."

The ordeal had really begun two-and-a-half months before. On June 30 Yaz homered off old friend Luis Tiant of the Yankees for a 3–2 Red Sox victory. That hit, in the season's 72nd game, was the 2,950th of his career. To his teammates it seemed certain that only those among them who held mid-August dates in the clubhouse pool on number 3,000 had a chance of collecting the $210 in the pot.

To Yaz's relief, and to the delight of the home fans, he collected his 3,000th hit at Fenway, just before the Sox hit the road.

But that day Yastrzemski's right Achilles tendon became inflamed and he limped through the second half of the season. By Wednesday night he was playing first base with spikes on his left foot and a sneaker on his right. When he came to bat in the ninth, he had hit only .220 since June 30. Yaz, 40, was looking it.

Hit number 2,999 had come on Sunday, Sept. 9, in his last at bat, so it seemed reasonable he would get the big one the next night. On Monday evening, scalpers were getting $50 a ticket on Yawkey Way, local pols came piling out of their limos, and as Yastrzemski stepped to the plate with two out in the first, everyone in Fenway Park stood and roared for him. A plane circled overhead flashing YAZ—3,000, and with each pitch from Baltimore's Dennis Martinez, thousands of flashbulbs flickered in the ballpark.

Well, the flashbulbs kept flickering, pitch after pitch, for three days and 13 at bats. Yastrzemski admitted that he was "anxious and swinging at pitches I normally would never swing at." On Tuesday he faced the Yankees and Tiant, whom Yaz calls "brother," and endured an 0-for-3 night.

Yastrzemski tried to pretend that none of this was getting to him. At 4:15 each afternoon he threw batting practice to his 17-year-old son Mike and performed his usual clubhouse pranks, but the strain on him and everyone around him was beginning to show. By Wednesday night scalpers were getting only $12 a seat. There were no planes overhead, and only two banners remained in the bleachers. Yaz's four children were missing school in Florida. They were part of a family entourage of 26 that Yaz kiddingly said was "making this the most expensive hit of my career—they're costing me $600 a day."

Catfish Hunter walked Yastrzemski his first time up Wednesday and was roundly booed for it. But the standing ovations for Yaz continued, even as he made outs his next three times up against Hunter and Jim Beattie. After hitting a grounder to second in the sixth, Yastrzemski had gone 0 for 10 with two walks, since 2,999; he was 1 for 18 and 13 for 78 in the countdown. If he failed in this game, he would have to face Ron Guidry the next night. If he missed then, he would have to wait a full week because Boston manager Don Zimmer had decided The Hit should come at home, and the Red Sox were about to embark on a seven-game road trip.

Beattie, who'd grown up in Portland, Maine, idolizing Yastrzemski, tried a fastball, and Yaz pulled it past Randolph and into rightfield. With that, bedlam.

POSTSCRIPT *Yastrzemski joined Willie Mays, Henry Aaron and Stan Musial as the only players to have 3,000 hits and 400 home runs (four more have since joined that club). He would play four additional seasons before retiring after 23 years with the Red Sox, finishing his career with 3,419 hits; as the 2012 campaign begins he is eighth on the alltime list.*

April 11, 1985
Dwight (Dewey) Evans drives it out of the
park against the Yankees, one of 379 homers
he hit in his 19 seasons with Boston
Photograph by CHUCK SOLOMON

1980
TO
1989

The Citgo sign is turned back on ~ Jim Rice comes to
the rescue ~ Yaz retires after 23 Red Sox seasons ~
Roger Clemens strikes out 20 Mariners

AP; DAN NERNEY (OPPOSITE)

1980

>>>>>

...U.S. OLYMPIC HOCKEY TEAM
WINS OLYMPICS GOLD...JOHN
LENNON IS MURDERED IN NEW
YORK..."WHO SHOT J.R."
EPISODE OF "DALLAS" IS MOST
WATCHED TV DRAMA EVER...

∧ JUNE 20

Light-hitting Angels shortstop
Freddie Patek hits three home
runs over the Green Monster in a
20-2 rout of the Red Sox

1981

>>>>>

...BASEBALL STRIKE DARKENS
BALLPARKS FOR SEVEN WEEKS...
52 HOSTAGES RELEASED IN IRAN
AFTER 444 DAYS...THE MTV
NETWORK DEBUTS...

‹ APRIL 10

Carlton Fisk returns to
Fenway on Opening Day
to make his debut with
the White Sox; he hits a
three-run homer off Bob
Stanley in the eighth in a
5-3 Chicago win

∧ APRIL 15

During a power outage
at Fenway, beloved public
address announcer Sherm
Feller uses a handheld
speaker to make
announcements. Feller
remains the voice of
Fenway for 26 years, from
1967 until '93, shortly
before he dies

SEPTEMBER 3 ›

The Red Sox and
Mariners play 20 innings and combine for 47 hits—Jerry Remy has six—in Seattle's 8-7 win. The game, lasting six hours and one minute, had to be completed the following day

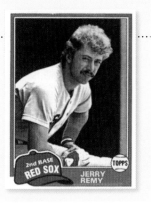

1982

›››››

. . . WORLD AIRWAYS FLIGHT 30 SKIDS OFF LOGAN RUNWAY INTO BOSTON HARBOR. . . NFL PLAYERS STRIKE FOR 57 DAYS. . . MICHAEL JACKSON'S "THRILLER" IS RELEASED . . .

MAY 1

Fenway hosts its first-
ever all-Red Sox Old Timers' Day and fans are thrilled to see players like Walt Dropo and Ted Williams. In the game, the Splendid Splinter goes 0 for 2, but a shoestring catch by the 63-year-old earns a standing ovation.

AUGUST 7 ›

Five-year-old Johnny
Keane is struck in the head by a foul ball off the bat of Sox infielder Dave Stapleton and is carried to an ambulance by outfielder Jim Rice. Despite a fractured skull, Keane recovers fully and throws out the Opening Day pitch in '83

TED GARTLAND/AP. JACQUELINE DUVOISIN (OPPOSITE)

1983

〉〉〉〉〉〉

. . . USFL, INCLUDING THE BOSTON
BREAKERS, DEBUTS WITH SPRING
FOOTBALL SCHEDULE . . . SALLY
RIDE IS FIRST U.S. WOMAN IN
SPACE . . . CHRYSLER INTRODUCES
THE MINIVAN . . .

AUGUST 10

The Citgo sign is illuminated, during
the seventh-inning stretch, for the first
time since 1979, when governor Edward
King had it turned off as an energy
conservation measure

SEPTEMBER 16

Boston manager Ralph Houk kicks at
umpire John Shulock after Wade Boggs
is called out at second base. Houk,
surprisingly, does not get the boot and
the Sox beat the Tigers 6-1

OCTOBER 1 〉

On "Yaz Day" at Fenway,
the retirement of Carl
Yastrzemski is feted; the next
day he will play his 3,308th
and final game for the Red Sox

1984

>>>>>>

...CELTICS BEAT THE LAKERS
TO WIN THEIR 15TH NBA TITLE...
APPLE MACINTOSH IS INTRODUCED
...RONALD REAGAN WINS
REELECTION IN LANDSLIDE OVER
WALTER MONDALE...

APRIL 17

NESN (New England Sports
Network) broadcasts its first
Red Sox game (versus Texas)
from Fenway on cable TV

MAY 28 ›

In ceremonies with Red Sox
president Jean Yawkey, Ted
Williams's number 9 and Joe
Cronin's number 4 are retired

^ JULY 6

The U.S. Olympic baseball
team, including a 19-year-old
first baseman named Mark
McGwire, plays an exhibition
game at Fenway

Excerpted from **SPORTS ILLUSTRATED 8.6.84**

BY STEVE WULF

UP AGAINST THE WALL

Having proved himself a worthy successor in the royal line of players who have ruled leftfield in Fenway Park, enigmatic Jim Rice still had not won all hearts and minds in Boston

IF YOU REALLY KNOW THE Wall—know how to use it to your advantage, appreciate its idiosyncrasies—it can be your friend. But since only a select few do know the leftfield wall at Boston's Fenway Park, it's called the Green Monster.

The same goes for Jim Rice, the Red Sox' leftfielder. There are friends who call Rice a warm, loving human being. If you don't know him, though, he can be as intimidating and inscrutable as a gargoyle. Says his friend, Ken Harrelson, who played and broadcast in Boston and currently works the mike for the White Sox, "Jim Ed is the most misunderstood person not just in baseball, but in my whole experience. I know Jekyll. A lot of people see Hyde."

This summer Red Sox fans are choosing up sides in The Great Debate: Can Boston afford to keep Rice, or can the franchise afford not to keep him? His contract will expire at the end of next year, but he wants a new one before the start of the '85 season, and he wants to be making about $2 million a year.

It's hard to believe the Fenway faithful would want to contemplate life without Rice, given his statistics and his age (31), but now on the various and voracious call-in radio shows in the Hub, they're saying that he doesn't hit in the clutch (though surely *some* of his 126 RBIs last year must have been important) and that the only major league record he'll break is for grounding into double plays. (With 26 already this season, he should easily pass former Red Sox outfielder Jackie Jensen, who set the standard with 32 in 1954.)

The love/hate relationship seems to come with the territory. Ted Williams had his splinter groups, and Carl Yastrzemski was alternately yazzed and razzed. Before Rice, they inhabited leftfield for almost 40 years—interrupted only by two wars, two Conigliaros, Juan Beniquez and Tommy Harper. But talent also comes with the territory. Since Fenway Park opened in

Rice had at least four MVP-caliber years for the Red Sox, but won the award only in '78.

1912, the composite batting average for regular leftfielders is an astounding .304. It's as if The Wall befriends them. The leftfielder in '18 and '19, by the way, was Babe Ruth.

Rice is a worthy successor, and an argument can be made that he is the most devastating hitter in baseball today. Yet he has remained lost in the shadows of Fred Lynn and Yaz on the Red Sox, and also behind several lesser superstars in baseball. Part of that is his own doing, though. He gets an F in media relations. "I just put the numbers on the board," he says. "That should be enough. It's tough enough playing every day, worrying about who's pitching and everything, so why worry about what's being written about you?" But he is getting sensitive about the double play business. After his double in the 10th beat California 4–3 last week, Rice brushed off reporters by saying,

"Why talk to me, I'm always hitting into double plays. What do I have now, 90?" The biggest shadow Rice has played in has been that of Yastrzemski, but that was lifted on the final day of the 1983 season. The game was Yaz's last, and everything he did was greeted with a standing ovation by the crowd at Fenway. But in the eighth inning, Rice walked to the plate, and the fans were on their feet again, changing the guard, crowning a new hero. Yaz was leading the cheers. "That felt very good," says Rice, who says no more about it.

"I wish I had a hundred dollars for every time I've talked to Jim about dealing with the press," says Harrelson. "I want the press to see what he's really like, to see him around children. Kids know better than anyone else if someone is good or bad, and kids love Jim Rice."

"I know you guys can't see it," says his friend Reggie Jackson, "but he's one of the best men I know. Here's a black man from South Carolina, thrown into a city like Boston. Talk about cultural, sociological shock. But don't try to tell that to anyone, because they'll tell you the man makes all that money, why can't he deal with it?"

Ask Rice if the fans have been warmer to him this year, and he says, "I don't think about things like that." Ask him about his contract, and he says, "I've got one year left on it, that's all." Ask him about his lack of recognition, and he says, "Why should it puzzle me? I've been doing a job for 10 years. I don't know what goes on in writers' minds."

The Rice most people know is the one who hits a home run and coolly trots around the bases, hardly acknowledging the cheers pouring down from the Fenway fans. Ralph Houk knows a different Rice. "He gets excited, all right," says the Boston manager. "The one way you can tell is by shaking his hand after a big home run. You really have to be careful he doesn't break your fingers. All his emotion, all his excitement is in that handshake."

1985

›››››

. . . BOSTON CHICKEN (LATER BOSTON MARKET) OPENS ITS FIRST STORE, IN NEWTON . . . JOHN KERRY IS SWORN IN AS U.S. SENATOR . . . PETE ROSE PASSES TY COBB AS ALLTIME HIT KING . . .

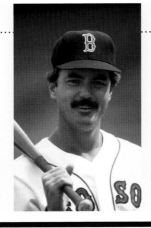

‹ **APRIL 11**

Dwight Evans hits a three- run homer to help beat the Yankees 6-4. A Fenway fixture in rightfield, "Dewey" plays 19 seasons in Boston

^
SEPTEMBER 21

Wade Boggs goes 2 for 5, raising his average to .374 and topping Tris Speaker's team record (222) for hits in a season; he will finish the year with 240 hits

1986

›››››

. . . LEN BIAS DIES TWO DAYS AFTER BEING DRAFTED BY CELTICS . . . SPACE SHUTTLE "CHALLENGER" EXPLODES . . . NINTENDO GAMES INTRODUCED IN THE U.S. . . . .

^
APRIL 29

As the Fenway crowd roars louder with each successive K, 23-year-old Roger Clemens strikes out 20 Seattle Mariners, setting a modern major league record

A PITCHER ON THE EDGE

In a good news-bad news season, Oil Can Boyd was a headliner

HE WAS EMOTIONAL, QUOTable and combustible, and Dennis (Oil Can) Boyd showed every bit of that volatility in 1986. En route to a career-best 16–10 season, Oil Can was a fixture in the Red Sox rotation, pitching behind Roger Clemens and Bruce Hurst. But in July, told that he'd not been selected to the All-Star team, the Can popped his top. Suspended by the Red Sox, Boyd was away for a month, including a stay for therapy in a hospital psychiatric ward.

He rebounded, resumed his role in the rotation, then set out on a roller coaster of a postseason. Boyd was the loser in Game 3 of the ALCS, but won a do-or-die Game 6 at Fenway—earning him a very high five from an appreciative fan *(left)*. In Game 3 of the World Series, Oil Can was lit up by the Mets, but had his sights set on dramatic redemption as the starter in Game 7. Alas, a rainout led Boston manager John McNamara to turn to Hurst instead. After the game, Oil Can broke down in tears.

MAY 17

The brothers DiMaggio—Vince, Dom and Joe—hold a rare family reunion, on the dugout steps at Fenway

OCTOBER 15

Pitcher Oil Can Boyd battles the California Angels for seven innings to lift the Red Sox to a 10-4 win in Game 6 of the ALCS, then takes congratulations from appreciative Fenway fans

OCTOBER 21

The Red Sox and Wade Boggs fall in Game 3 of the '86 series to the Mets and Keith Hernandez, but after winning Game 5 leave Fenway with a three games to two lead—only to go to Shea Stadium in New York and lose dramatically in the final two games

1987

›››››

. . . NFL PLAYERS UNION STRIKES, REPLACEMENT PLAYERS APPEAR IN THREE GAMES . . . DOW JONES AVERAGE PLUNGES 508 POINTS, A 22.6% LOSS . . . "THE SIMPSONS" DEBUTS AS A SHORT ON "THE TRACEY ULLMAN SHOW" . . .

‹ JULY 24

Still scarred nine months after his Game 6, game-ending error in the World Series, Boston first baseman Bill Buckner cleans out his Fenway locker a day after being told he's been put on waivers

1988

›››››

. . . NAACP SUES BOSTON HOUSING AUTHORITY OVER SEGREGATED HOUSING . . . CHICAGO CUBS PLAY FIRST NIGHT GAME AT WRIGLEY FIELD . . . OVER ONE-THIRD OF YELLOWSTONE NATIONAL PARK IS DESTROYED BY FIRES . . .

DECEMBER 1

In a major renovation of Fenway, a new press box and the 600 Club seating area are built. The club is later renamed the .406 Club in honor of Ted Williams

1989

›››››

. . . MAGNITUDE 7.1 EARTHQUAKE DISRUPTS GIANTS-A'S WORLD SERIES . . . BERLIN WALL IS TORN DOWN . . . "FIELD OF DREAMS" OPENS IN THEATERS . . .

SEPTEMBER 1

Reliever Bob Stanley pitches the final 1²⁄₃ innings in a 7-2 Red Sox loss to the Mariners; it is Stanley's 321st and final appearance at Fenway, more than any pitcher in the park's history

1990
TO
1999

Jean Yawkey dies ~ Haywood Sullivan sells ~
Gigantic Coke bottles appear over Fenway
~ The All-Star game returns to Boston

September 29, 1990
Wade Boggs, hitting over .300 at the time as is his custom,
takes aim at Fenway's bleachers in batting practice.
Photograph by HEINZ KLUETMEIER

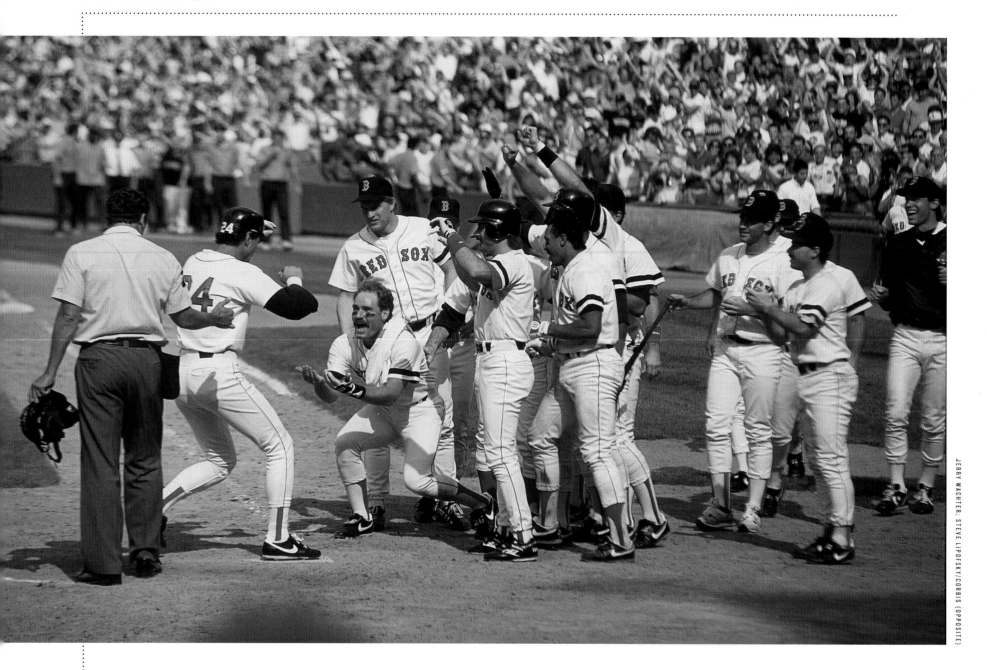

JERRY WACHTER; STEVE LIPOFSKY/CORBIS (OPPOSITE)

1990

>>>>>

*...SOUTH AFRICA'S NELSON
MANDELA IS RELEASED FROM
PRISON...MIT PROFESSOR
TIM BERNERS-LEE CREATES THE
WORLD-WIDE WEB..."SEINFELD"
SERIES DEBUTS ON NBC...*

JUNE 6 ›

Nearly 12 years after his home run
tormented the Red Sox, Bucky Dent,
manager of the Yankees, is fired at
Fenway just before his club loses 4-1
to fall 9½ games behind Boston. For
Sox fans, the retribution is sweet

^
APRIL 17

Fenway hosts the first
Baseball Beanpot Tournament.
In the final on the 19th, BC beats
Harvard 6-3. Attendance: 594

^
JUNE 23

With his second home run of the
game, this one a walk-off winner in
the 10th inning, Dwight Evans beats
the Orioles 4-3. Wade Boggs leads a
crew of Sox waiting at home

FENWAY PARK

OCTOBER 3 ›

Tom Brunansky, having already hit a triple, a single and driven in a run, makes a spectacular, game-saving sliding catch in rightfield on a liner off the bat of Chicago's Ozzie Guillen. The catch, with two out in the ninth, and the 3-1 win send the Red Sox to the playoffs

OCTOBER 6

The ALCS opens in Fenway, Boston vs. Oakland. Alas for the Red Sox, the national anthem before Game 1 represents their high point as they're swept by the A's. The Sox score exactly one run in each of the four games

1991

›››››

. . . MAGIC JOHNSON ANNOUNCES HE HAS TESTED POSITIVE FOR HIV, RETIRES FROM LAKERS . . . SOVIET UNION FORMALLY DISSOLVES . . . SEATTLE BAND NIRVANA RELEASES "SMELLS LIKE TEEN SPIRIT," STARTS GRUNGE MOVEMENT . . .

OCTOBER 8

Joe Morgan is fired as Boston manager, replaced by Butch Hobson. Says Morgan, "This team just isn't that good"

CHANGING ITS TUNE

The vibe at Fenway has been altered by the sounds of The Lovin' Spoonful, Neil Diamond, Three Dog Night and the Dropkick Murphys

AFTER THE BOTTOM OF the second inning on a June evening in 1992, with the Red Sox already down 5–2 to the Tigers, the Fenway faithful heard a foreign sound coming from the p.a. speakers: rock 'n roll, baby. Instead of the organ fare that had long monopolized the park, The Lovin' Spoonful's *Summer in the City* shook the joint, followed that night by other numbers, including the Monkees' *I'm a Believer* (which apparently did not inspire the Red Sox who went on to lose 8–3). It was a Fenway first.

Since that night, songs and the Sox have combined in sonic traditions, most famously Neil Diamond's *Sweet Caroline* played each eighth inning since 2002, and the triumphant trio of *Dirty Water*, *Tessie* and Three Dog Night's *Joy to the World* following every Boston win.

At least one Fenway veteran, however, did not embrace The Lovin' Spoonful that night; longtime Sox organist John Kiley, who played from 1953 until his '90 retirement, said afterward, "I didn't like it. Something about it didn't seem to fit into a ball game." Kiley died a year later, spared the sound of *I'm Shipping Up to Boston* by the Dropkick Murphys *(below)* every time closer Jonathan Papelbon sprints in from the bullpen.

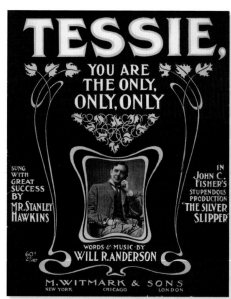

MICHAEL IVINS/BOSTON RED SOX; TRANSCENDENTAL GRAPHICS (TESSIE); SUSAN WALSH/AP (OPPOSITE)

1992

>>>>>>

...RIOTS HIT L.A. AFTER POLICE ACQUITTED OF RODNEY KING BEATING...TORONTO BLUE JAYS ARE FIRST NON-U.S.-BASED TEAM TO WIN WORLD SERIES...JOHNNY CARSON LEAVES "THE TONIGHT SHOW" AFTER THREE DECADES...

‹ FEBRUARY 26

Jean Yawkey dies at 83. She leaves no heirs, thus Fenway is without a Yawkey as caretaker for the first time in 59 years

JUNE 15 ›

Boston's Jeff Reardon gets the Yankees' Kevin Maas to strike out swinging, earning his 342nd career save and passing Rollie Fingers to set a new major league record

^ JUNE 29

For the first time in Fenway's history, rock music is heard through the public address system at a Red Sox game; before this, all music had been provided by the stadium organ. The first tune to play: *Summer in the City* by The Lovin' Spoonful

SEPTEMBER 24

"Father" Guido Sarducci of
Saturday Night Live performs
an exorcism of the Curse of the
Bambino outside the park, along
with 104 "altar girls"

1993

〉〉〉〉〉〉

. . . BRANCH DAVIDIAN CULT
MEMBERS ARE KILLED IN WACO,
TEXAS . . . BOSTON MAYOR
RAY FLYNN BECOMES U.S.
AMBASSADOR TO VATICAN . . .
AEROSMITH'S "GET A GRIP" IS
NO. 1 SONG . . .

NOVEMBER 23

Haywood Sullivan sells his share of the
Red Sox for an estimated $36–$45 million,
a profit of at least $35 million profit on
his $1 million 1978 investment. During
Sullivan's tenure, Boston goes 1,237-1,134

1994

〉〉〉〉〉〉

. . . MURDER SUSPECT O.J.
SIMPSON, IN WHITE FORD
BRONCO, IS CHASED BY POLICE
. . . BASEBALL PLAYERS GO ON
STRIKE IN AUGUST, CANCELING
WORLD SERIES . . . SOUTH BOSTON
MOBSTER WHITEY BULGER GOES
INTO HIDING . . .

APRIL 4

With a proposal looming for
a new ballpark to be built
on the other side of Yawkey
Way, the Fenway faithful pack
the old yard, many of them
opposed to the project

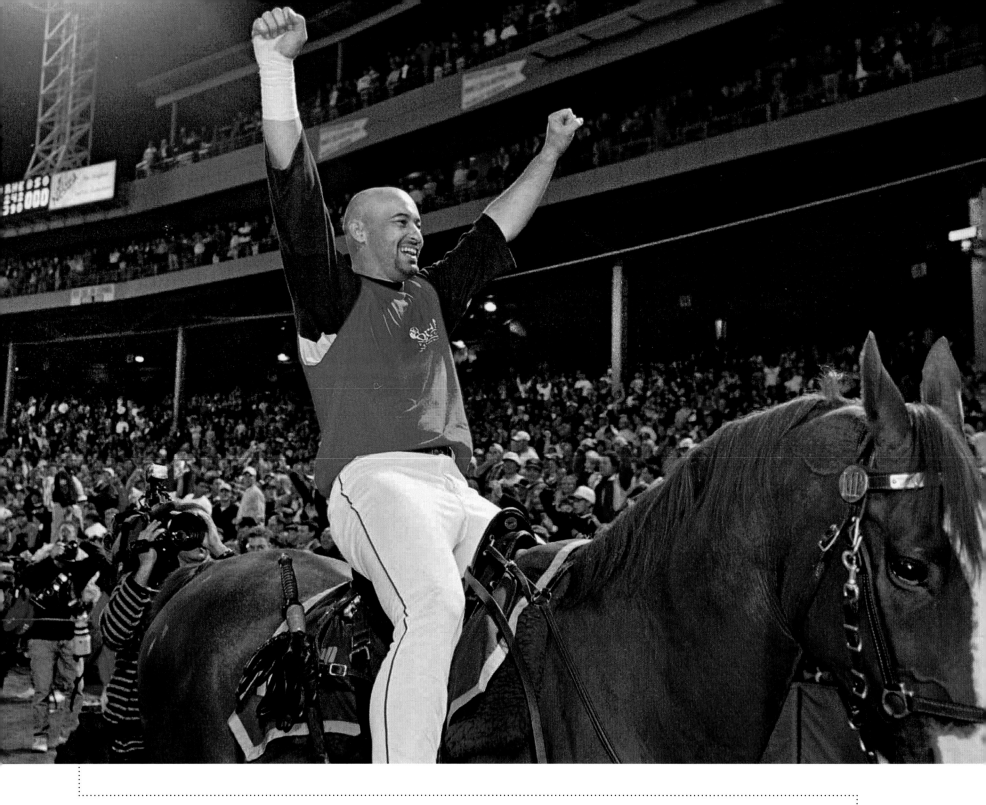

1995

›››››››

. . . TED WILLIAMS TUNNEL OPENS
BENEATH BOSTON HARBOR . . . CAL
RIPKEN JR. PASSES LOU GEHRIG'S
2,130 CONSECUTIVE GAMES
PLAYED, IS ALLTIME IRON MAN . . .
GRATEFUL DEAD'S JERRY GARCIA
HAS FATAL HEART ATTACK . . .

310

^

APRIL 26

The distance-marker at the
leftfield foul pole, previously
315, now reads 310 after being
remeasured before the season

APRIL 26 ›

Jose Canseco, with his
nearly $6 million salary,
makes his Fenway debut.
Despite the hype, he's
gone two years later

^

SEPTEMBER 20

The Red Sox beat the Brewers 3–2
to clinch the AL East, after which
outfielder Mike Greenwell leads the
Fenway crowd in cheers from atop a
police horse

DAMIAN STROHMEYER; WINSLOW TOWNSON/AP (OPPOSITE)

1996

››››››

...TIGER WOODS TURNS PRO, WINS TWO OF FIVE EVENTS HE PLAYS...TED KACZYNSKI, FORMER HARVARD CHILD PRODIGY, IS ARRESTED AS UNABOMBER...CHESS COMPUTER "DEEP BLUE" DEFEATS WORLD CHAMPION GARRY KASPAROV...

˄ MAY 5

The Boston bullpen keeps waiting for the call as starter Tim Wakefield gives up 11 runs on 10 hits to the Blue Jays

JUNE 6 ›

Red Sox shortstop John Valentin (middle) hits for the cycle; no Red Sox player has matched that feat at Fenway since

‹ SEPTEMBER 24

Mo Vaughn blasts three home runs in a game for the first time in his career; the third bomb is also his 200th hit of the season. Afterwards, he says, "Mo Vaughn is more than a home run hitter. I like to think of myself as a hitter."

1997

›››››

...IRISH REPUBLICAN ARMY
DECLARES CEASE FIRE IN
NORTHERN IRELAND...HEAD
OF THE CHARLES REGATTA
BECOMES A TWO-DAY EVENT...
BASEBALL LEGEND HARRY CARAY
BROADCASTS HIS LAST GAME...

^ APRIL 1

A Spring blizzard dumps 18 inches of snow on Boston; 10 days later the home opener at Fenway is played as scheduled

‹ APRIL 10

Opening Day reveals three 25-foot-high Coke bottles atop a leftfield light tower. Writes Dan Shaughnessy in *The Boston Globe*, "Purists will be sickened."

^ APRIL 13

New mascot Wally The Green Monster, unveiled before the season, throws out the first pitch on Opening Day; he's a hit with kids

DAMIAN STROHMEYER; STEVEN SENNE/AP (OPPOSITE)

‹ JULY 12 ›

Roger Clemens makes his first appearance at Fenway since signing with the Blue Jays; to the dismay of derisive fans, he strikes out 16 to beat his old team

DECEMBER 12 ›

Reigning NL Cy Young winner Pedro Martinez has a Fenway press conference to announce his $75 million deal with the Sox

1998

››››››

. . . MARK MCGWIRE HITS 70 HOME RUNS; SAMMY SOSA HAS 66 . . . BILL CLINTON IS IMPEACHED BY HOUSE OF REPRESENTATIVES FOR PERJURY AND OBSTRUCTION OF JUSTICE, THEN ACQUITTED . . . "TITANIC" BECOMES HIGHEST GROSSING FILM EVER . . .

SEPTEMBER 3

A nonprofit organization, Save Fenway Park!, is established to counter rumored plans by Sox brass to build a new park

Excerpted from SPORTS ILLUSTRATED 4.20.98

BY GERRY CALLAHAN

IN LOVE WITH THE NEW GUY

For beleaguered Red Sox fans, the arrival of pitcher Pedro Martinez was cause for delight. And the new ace's huge new contract raised their hopes that fortunes were changing

AS HE STEPPED OUTSIDE OF Fenway Park and into the players' parking lot after the Red Sox home opener Friday night, Pedro Martinez laughed aloud at all the outstretched arms poking from under the bottom of the security fence as if they were reaching from the grave. These resourceful fans wanted an opportunity to shake the new star's hand, even if they couldn't see his face. Baseballs and trading cards came sliding out as well, and Martinez signed each one and slid it back. "It's part of my life," he says. He vows to never refuse an autograph or an interview request and promises to embrace the stifling pressure that waits around every turn for the new ace of the Boston staff, especially an ace making more money than any player in baseball history. "He loves everything about it," says Franklin Jaime, Martinez's cousin, who lives in Providence. "This is the way he wants it. To him, this is what baseball should be like."

As soon as they got a glimpse of him heading to his car, a raucous mob of Red Sox fans broke into the chant "Pe-dro! Pe-dro!" despite the fact that the game had ended nearly two hours earlier and the temperature was 37°. That brought a smile to Martinez's face. "There was always something missing in Montreal," he says of his prior baseball home. "To be here and play for people who eat, drink and sleep baseball, that makes me feel good. I think this is a special place."

It is now. Every fifth day.

When Martinez first arrived in Boston in December, a couple hundred fans met him at the airport, cheering wildly and chanting his name as if he were some kind of rebel leader in charge of a surprise Red Sox resurgence. This was 2½ months after the Red Sox had finished 20 games out of first and a long, cold winter away from reporting day for pitchers and catchers. This was all Martinez had to see.

Martinez was as happy with the baseball-crazy Boston fans as they were with him. "This is a special place," he said.

"They were yelling and waving flags, and someone had a sign that said WE LOVE YOU, PEDRO," says Martinez, who had been traded to the Red Sox on Nov. 18. "That night I said to someone, 'I think I love Boston already.'" He loved it a lot more a day later when he signed a six-year, $75 million contract. And now Boston's love has only intensified.

Even before he moved into an apartment across the river in Cambridge, Martinez was a splash of color on Boston's stodgy-gray baseball landscape, a proud Latin pitcher who shared an intense passion for the game with the fans in his new hometown. "That's why I knew he'd fit in so well," says Red Sox pitching coach Joe Kerrigan. "The atmosphere here is similar to the Dominican Republic [where Martinez is from]. Boston has the same passion and love for the game, and I knew he'd appreciate that."

Martinez made his Fenway debut Saturday against the Seattle Mariners in an April game that came equipped with an October buzz. Hall of Famer Juan Marichal, who played briefly in Boston at the end of his career, flew up from his home in the Dominican Republic to see his countryman's Boston premiere. Also on hand was Luis Tiant, a native of Cuba and a Boston legend thanks to his heroics for the pennant-winning Red Sox of 1975. Martinez called them "the two greatest Latin American pitchers ever." They were joined by hundreds of jubilant fans from various Latin communities around New England, making staid old Fenway look like a colorful World Cup venue. Many of Martinez's admirers waved Dominican flags and celebrated every strike their hero threw.

"He just loves to pitch in front of a packed house, with everyone standing, watching him work," says first baseman Mo Vaughn. "I think he's going to thrive here." (Vaughn himself remains unsigned after this season, and his contract negotiation has evolved into a daily stare-down with Boston general manager Dan Duquette, who engineered the trade with Montreal for Martinez).

Against the Mariners at Fenway, Martinez was dominant. With a dazzling combination of variable velocity and pinpoint location, and an array of fastballs and sliders to go with perhaps the best changeup in the league, Martinez allowed just two singles and struck out 12 en route to a 5–0 shutout victory. His $75 million price tag suddenly seemed almost reasonable.

As Martinez drove out of the team parking lot, a large group of fans broke into a loud chorus of "Sign Mo! Sign Mo!" He stopped his car, rolled down the window, pumped his fist into the cold air and joined in the chant, "Sign Mo! Sign Mo!" In the car behind Martinez, Duquette just shook his head and smiled. Just what he needed. Another crazed Boston baseball fan trying to tell him what to do.

1999

>>>>>>

. . . FIFTEEN DIE IN SHOOTINGS AT COLUMBINE HIGH SCHOOL IN COLORADO . . . TEAM USA WINS RYDER CUP AT THE COUNTRY CLUB IN BROOKLINE . . . JOHN KENNEDY JR. AND WIFE DIE IN PLANE CRASH NEAR MARTHA'S VINEYARD . . .

MAY 15

Red Sox CEO John Harrington announces, as preservationists feared, a plan to build a new park near Fenway

MAY 10 >

Nomar Garciaparra hits three homers, including two grand slams; his 10 RBIs match a Fenway record shared by Norm Zauchin and Reggie Jackson

JULY 13

At the All-Star Game, Fenway's third, Ted Williams, 80 and virtually blind, throws out the first pitch with the aid of Tony Gwynn

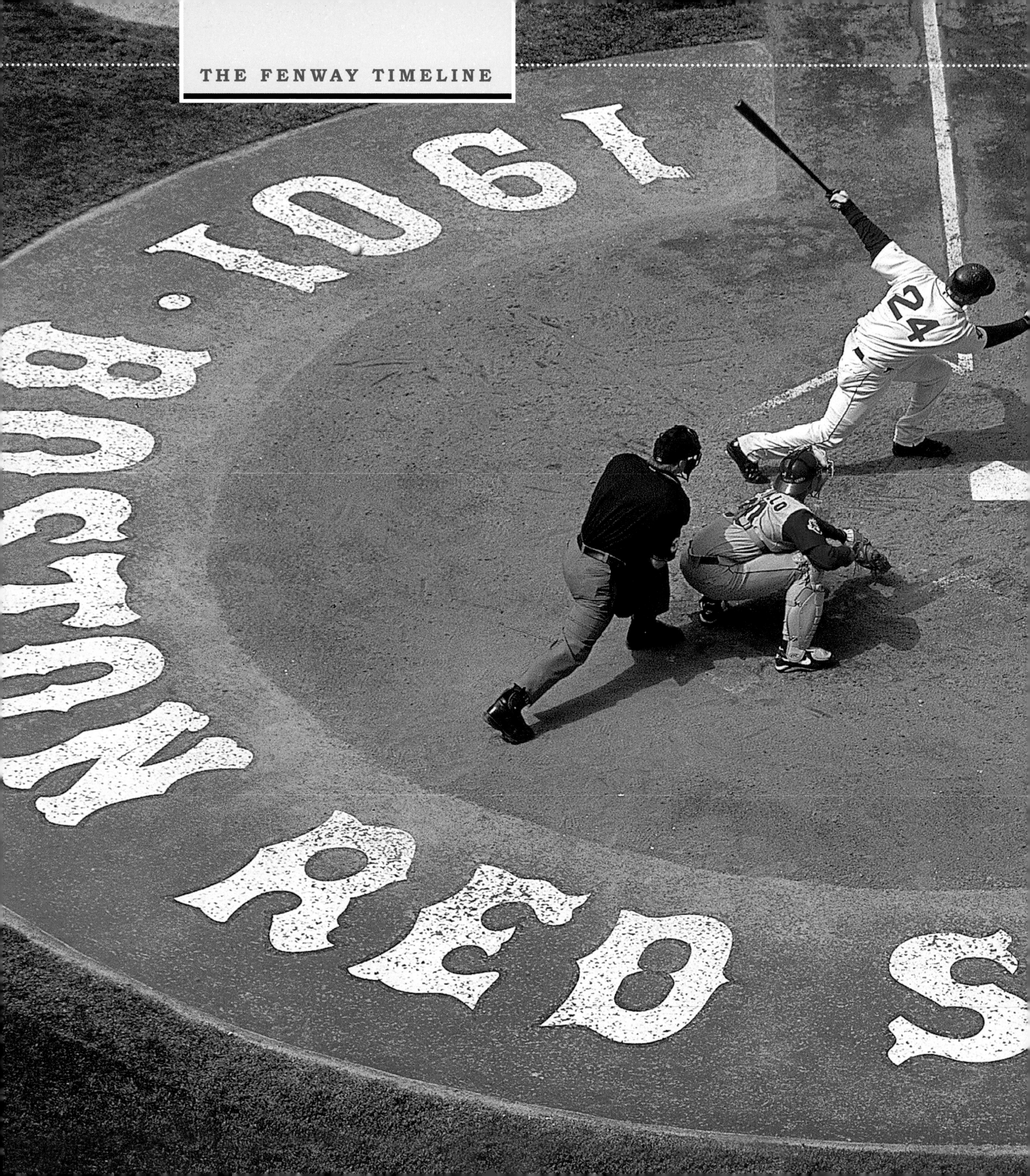
1901
BOSTON
RED S
24

2000
TO
2011

The Red Sox win two World Series ~ Fenway gets updated with a major renovation ~ The Bruins and the NHL bring hockey to Fenway

May 26, 2001
In his first Red Sox season, Manny Ramirez bats against Toronto. He will finish the year with 41 homers and 125 RBIs.
Photograph by CHUCK SOLOMON

2000

>>>>>>

. . . WITH 199TH PICK OF NFL DRAFT, PATRIOTS SELECT TOM BRADY . . . SUPREME COURT DECLARES GEORGE W. BUSH WINNER OF PRESIDENTIAL ELECTION OVER AL GORE . . . ONLINE GIANT AOL BUYS TIME WARNER FOR $165 BILLION . . .

< **MAY 13**

TV series *The Practice* shoots season finale wedding scene at Fenway, with stars Kelli Williams and Dylan McDermott

SEPTEMBER 4 >

Carlton Fisk, New England– born and bred and recently elected to Hall of Fame, has his number 27 retired at Fenway

2001

>>>>>>

. . . HIJACKERS CRASH PLANES INTO WORLD TRADE CENTER AND PENTAGON . . . FEDERAL COURT RULES AGAINST NAPSTER ON MUSIC SHARING . . . RICK PITINO RESIGNS AS CELTICS COACH . . .

JIM BOURG/REUTERS; CHUCK SOLOMON (OPPOSITE)

^
AUGUST 3

Heavy rains flood the tunnel
between the dugout and the
clubhouse forcing Red Sox
batboys to rescue the lumber

DECEMBER 20

The Red Sox and Fenway
Park are sold to a group led by
John Henry. Price (including
80% of NESN): $660 million

APRIL 6

A 24-foot high, 68-foot-
wide illuminated John Hancock
sign is unveiled above the
centerfield scoreboard

MAY 26

Fenway groundskeepers go
all-out, mowing a bat and ball
into the outfield and a pair of
sox at the pitcher's mound

AUGUST 6 ›

Sox catcher Scott Hatteberg
is the first player in history to
hit into a triple play and hit a
grand slam in the same game

2002

›››››

. . . ADAM VINATIERI FIELD GOAL
GIVES PATRIOTS THEIR FIRST SUPER
BOWL TITLE . . . DEPARTMENT
OF HOMELAND SECURITY IS
ESTABLISHED . . . STEVE FOSSETT
IS FIRST TO SOLO-CIRCUMNAVIGATE
GLOBE IN A BALLOON . . .

‹ **APRIL 1**

Lombardi trophy, and
champion Patriots, including
Lawyer Milloy and Tom Brady,
visit Fenway on Opening Day

APRIL 27 ›

The Red Sox' Derek Lowe
throws the first no-hitter at
Fenway in 37 years, shutting
down Tampa Bay 10-0

^
JULY 22

Ted Williams is eulogized
by, among others, legendary
broadcaster Ned Martin; the
next day, Martin dies at 78

THE FENWAY THROWDOWN

Of all the episodes in the Red Sox-Yankees rivalry, this one was surely the most bizarre

THINGS GOT WEIRD IN A hurry during Game 3 of the ALCS. It began in the top of the fourth when Boston starter Pedro Martinez hit Yankees outfielder Karim Garcia in the head with a fastball. Garcia then slid hard into Sox second baseman Todd Walker to break up a double play, inciting a shoving match as both benches cleared. Order was restored—for a moment.

Before the bottom half of the inning, umpires warned Yanks righty (and former Sox ace) Roger Clemens against any retaliation. Nice try. In the first at bat, Clemens threw at Manny Ramirez, just missing his head. Ramirez pointed his bat and yelled at Clemens as the benches emptied again. Immediately, 72-year-old Yankees bench coach (and former Sox manager) Don Zimmer burst from the Yankees dugout and ran directly at Martinez, who was standing outside the Boston dugout. As the charging Zimmer reached him, Martinez sidestepped, grabbed the coach by the back of his head, and shoved him to the ground. Zimmer tumbled, landing facedown. After several minutes, Zimmer walked off the field, uninjured, and was seen later laughing in the dugout.

Weird? No one was ejected from the game.

CHRIS FAYTOK/THE STAR-LEDGER/REUTERS; WINSLOW TOWNSON (OPPOSITE)

2003

\>\>\>\>\>\>

. . . AARON BOONE'S 11TH INNING HOME RUN IN YANKEE STADIUM IN ALCS GAME 7 CRUSHES RED SOX . . . SCIENTISTS MAP ENTIRE HUMAN GENOME . . . ZAKIM BRIDGE COMPLETED IN DOWNTOWN BOSTON . . .

APRIL 12

National League scores are added to scoreboard for first time since '75; ads are added to wall for first time since '46

NATIONAL LEAGUE						
R	P		IN	R		P
3	35	PIT				18
2	51	HOU				33
2	40	ATL				35

AUGUST 22

Pregame lightning appears to strike the nearby Prudential Tower; but the game goes on: Sox 6, Mariners 4

SEPTEMBER 6 >

Bruce Springsteen gives Fenway its first hard rock concert and promises a "rock 'n' roll exorcism" of the Curse

OCTOBER 11

In the midst of a brawl, Pedro Martinez grabs Yankees coach (and former Boston manager) Don Zimmer and hurls him, facefirst, into the Fenway turf

DAMIAN STROHMEYER (2)

2004

〉〉〉〉〉〉

... MARK ZUCKERBERG DESIGNS
FACEBOOK IN HARVARD DORM
ROOM ... INDIAN OCEAN TSUNAMI
KILLS MORE THAN 200,000 ...
NHL PLAYERS ARE LOCKED OUT
AND SEASON IS CANCELED ...

JULY 24

Endearing himself to Fenway
fans forever, Jason Varitek
shoves his glove into the face
of Alex Rodriguez. The fight
begins when A-Rod is hit by
a pitch from Bronson Arroyo;
A-Rod barks at Varitek who
responds with the facial. Boston,
8½ games behind Yanks in the
standings at the time, wins the
game 11-10, then goes 45-20 en
route to the World Series

‹ SEPTEMBER 16

The film *Fever Pitch* is shot
at Fenway; in one scene
actress Drew Barrymore runs
past outfielder Johnny Damon,
played by Johnny Damon

OCTOBER 8 ›

After his walk-off home run
wins Game 3 to sweep the
Angels in the ALDS, David Ortiz
is mobbed at home plate

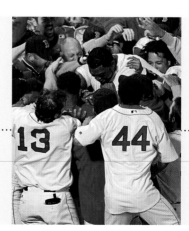

Excerpted from SPORTS ILLUSTRATED 10.25.04 *and* 11.10.04

BY TOM VERDUCCI

THE PLAY THAT CHANGED IT ALL

Its ultimate importance could be seen only in retrospect, but when pinch runner Dave Roberts stole second base in the ninth inning of Game 4 of the ALCS at Fenway, the worm turned

ALL OF IT—THE GREATEST comeback in sports history, the manhandling of the Yankees mystique, the vanquishing of that massive inferiority complex, the triumph of idiocy—began with a wink.

The Red Sox were clinically dead on Oct. 17: three outs from being swept in the American League Championship Series with the great Mariano Rivera on the mound for New York in the ninth inning of Game 4 at Fenway Park, Yankees leading 4–3. When Rivera walked leadoff batter Kevin Millar on five pitches, Boston manager Terry Francona ordered Dave Roberts to run for Millar. Roberts bounded up the rubber-topped steps of the home dugout, and as he crossed the custom-dyed, red dirt warning track, he peered over his left shoulder at Francona. Their eyes met for an instant, and Francona gave him a wink.

The men on a baseball club, by virtue of their incessant travel, spend so much time together that the unspoken can be as clear as the spoken. Roberts knew what the wink meant: He was free to steal second base.

"That just shows you about Terry and the confidence he has in us," Roberts said. "To give me the green light in the ninth inning of an elimination game against the best team in baseball . . . wow!"

Facing Bill Mueller as he tried to protect the one-run lead, Rivera threw first not to the plate but over to first base, and then again. And again. As a base stealer Roberts is a Phi Beta Kappa student of pitchers and their tendencies and mannerisms, so as Rivera came set again and made his first movement, Roberts knew instantly that Rivera was delivering a pitch to Mueller and took off for second. With that quick jump, Roberts swiped the base just ahead of the tag by Yankees shortstop Derek Jeter.

Three days later Red Sox pitcher Derek Lowe would stand in the low-ceilinged, tiny visiting

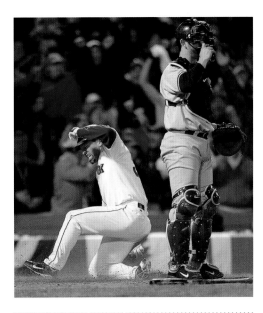

After his bold steal of second, Roberts scored the game-tying run and kept Boston hopes alive.

clubhouse of Yankee Stadium, a hothouse thick with cigar smoke and champagne spray, and proclaim, "The biggest play of this series was Dave Roberts stealing the base in Game 4."

Mueller had taken the pitch on which Roberts had stolen for a ball. He squared to bunt on the next pitch but took it for a strike. Francona decided to take the bunt off, figuring the New York corner infielders were now pinched in for a bunt, reducing their range, and that Mueller could at least pull the ball to the right to get Roberts to third, or at best drive him in with a hit. The manager's best-case scenario became reality. Mueller whacked the next pitch past a desperate Rivera, who vainly sprawled like a hockey goalie to keep the shot from whizzing into centerfield. "I definitely thought he was bunting [on the third pitch]," Rivera said later. "But I walked the first guy. That was the key." Roberts sped home with the run that tied the game and turned the series.

When the ALCS had arrived in Boston for Game 3, the Red Sox were already down two games to none, having lost 10–7 and 3–1 in New York. But nobody in the Boston locker room was showing much concern.

"We've dug ourselves a hole," centerfielder Johnny Damon said, "but even idiots know how to dig themselves out of the hole."

The Red Sox reveled in their self-styled role as idiots. They played fast and loose, sporting assorted arrangements of facial hair. Salsa music and television sets blared in their clubhouse before games. "They're a bunch of characters," Francona said, "but they have character."

The Yankees and the Red Sox then proceeded to stage a trilogy of extraordinary games over consecutive evenings before three packed houses at Fenway, each game longer and more excruciating than the one before. The two teams combined for 15 hours, 11 minutes of baseball in which 1,299 pitches would be thrown and the managers would make 29 pitching changes. At times it defied belief.

Yet it hardly looked memorable after Game 3 when New York took glorified batting practice in a record 19–8 blowout of the Sox. But then Roberts ignited the Game 4 comeback with his ninth-inning larceny against Rivera. Three innings later, when the last of the 11 pitchers used in the game threw the last of the 394 pitches in the last of the 302 minutes elapsed, Boston slugger David Ortiz won it with a bolt to rightfield, a two-run, 12th-inning homer off Paul Quantrill at the ridiculously late hour of 1:22 a.m. EDT on Monday. The Red Sox became the first team since the 1910 Chicago Cubs to stave off a four-game sweep with an extra-inning win. "Hey, it's one game," a weary Rivera said after the 6–4 loss. "We've got another one tomorrow. . . . Actually, today."

But once the series tilted in Boston's favor, the rest was inevitable, almost like a mud slide. The ALCS had changed in the blink of an eye.

OCTOBER 23 ›

On his way to a .412 average in the World Series, Manny Ramirez goes 3 for 5 with two RBIs in Game 1; Sox win 11–9

OCTOBER 24

Still bleeding from a sutured Achilles tendon (already having famously endured the injury in New York to win Game 6 of the ALCS), Curt Schilling takes the mound in Game 2 of the World Series. He goes six innings in Boston's 6–2 win over St. Louis

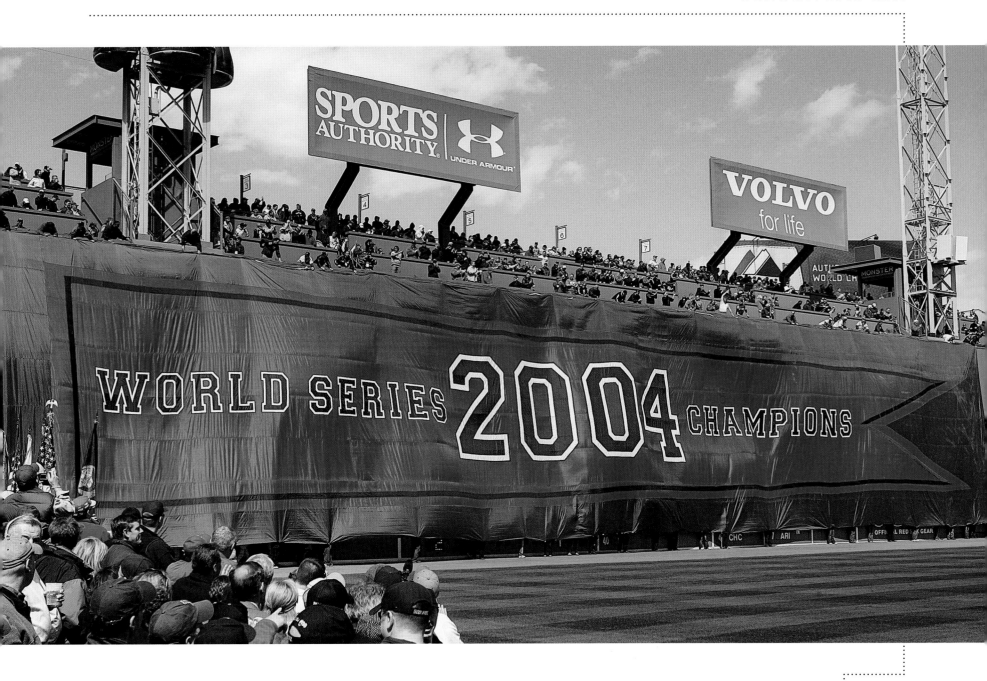

NOVEMBER 1 >

Mark Bellhorn, the hero of Game 1 of the World Series with his eighth-inning two-run homer, is on the cover of SI

DECEMBER 6 >>

The Red Sox, winners of five of six postseason games at Fenway and their first title in 86 years, are named SI's Sportsmen of the Year

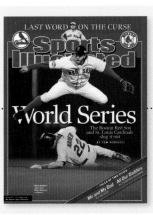

2005

>>>>>>

...HURRICANE KATRINA DEVASTATES NEW ORLEANS... BOSTON COLLEGE LEAVES BIG EAST FOR ACC... CHICAGO WHITE SOX WIN THE WORLD SERIES FOR FIRST TIME SINCE 1917...

APRIL 11

On Opening Day, a massive championship banner is unfurled on the Green Monster and rings are bestowed

JUNE 1 ›

Before a game against the Orioles, Red Sox pitcher Mike Timlin tapes a "crime scene" profile of Johnny Damon at the spot where Damon hit the wall while chasing a fly ball in the game the night before

JULY 16 ›

Boston G.M. Theo Epstein and pitcher Tim Wakefield perform at Fenway in a benefit concert. Sox pitcher Bronson Arroyo also gets in some licks during the evening

AUGUST 21

The Rolling Stones launch their "Bigger Bang Tour" at Fenway. Says Mick Jagger to the crowd of 30,000: "Boston is a championship city, you know? . . . We're going to try to hit one over the Green Monster." (The warmup act is The Black-Eyed Peas)

WINSLOW TOWNSON; KEVIN MAZUR/WIREIMAGE.COM (OPPOSITE)

SEPTEMBER 28

Chewbacca and Princess Leia of *Star Wars* throw out the first pitch to promote an exhibit at the Boston Museum of Science. The southpaw Chewie fires a decent fastball, catching just a little dirt in the lefty batting box

2006

〉〉〉〉〉〉

. . . GOVERNOR MITT ROMNEY'S REFORM BILL MANDATES HEALTH INSURANCE FOR NEARLY ALL MASSACHUSETTS RESIDENTS . . . RED SOX REHIRE G.M. THEO EPSTEIN THREE MONTHS AFTER HE RESIGNS . . . "THE DEPARTED" HITS MOVIE SCREENS, WILL WIN BEST PICTURE OSCAR . . .

JULY 8

The Dave Matthews Band performs two sold-out shows at Fenway, duly noted by the Green Monster scoreboard

SEPTEMBER 26

The season of David Ortiz (above hitting an earlier dinger) reaches its zenith when he hits his last homer of the year, his 54th, a Red Sox single-season record

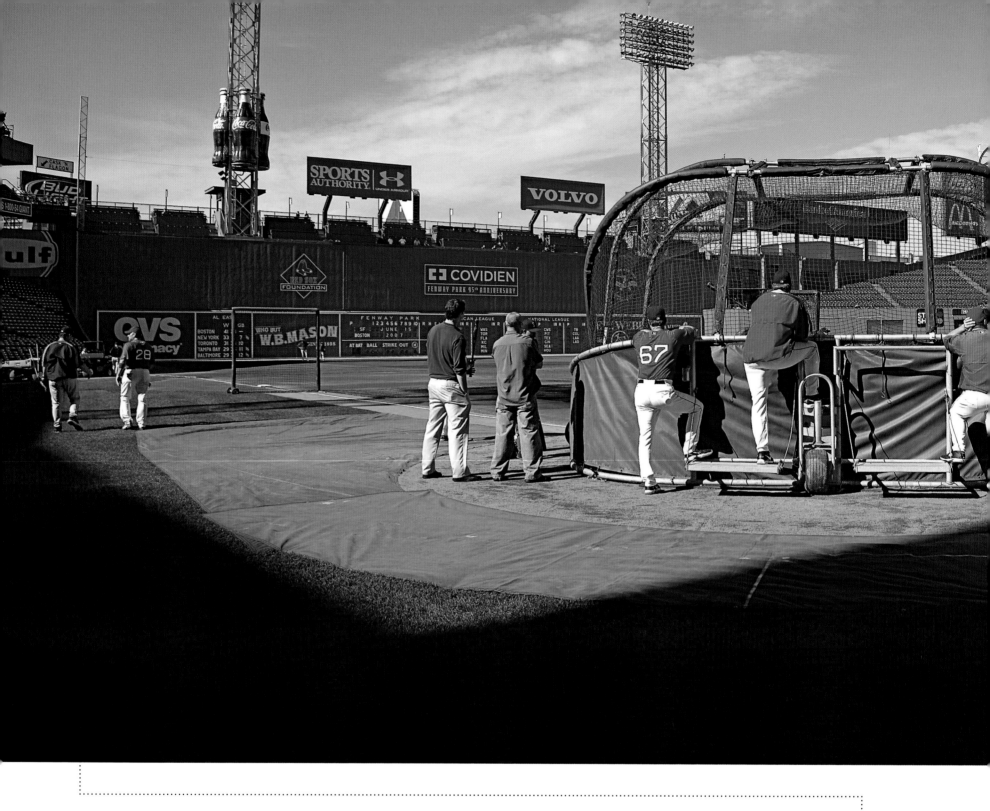

2007

››››››

... THE PATRIOTS COMPLETE THE
NFL'S FIRST 16-0 UNDEFEATED
REGULAR SEASON ... APPLE
RELEASES THE FIRST IPHONE
IN THE U.S ... BOSTON TUNNEL
PROJECT "THE BIG DIG" IS
FINISHED ...

‹ APRIL 10

Members of the 1967
"Impossible Dream" team—
Yaz, Hawk, Rico, et al—reunite
at Fenway, 40 years after

APRIL 10 ›

A Dunkin' Donuts sign in
Japanese ("Welcome to
Fenway Park") greets new Sox
pitcher Daisuke Matsuzaka

^
JUNE 15

The Red Sox warm up their
bats in the practice cage; the
work pays off when they batter
the San Francisco Giants 10-2

CHUCK SOLOMON; WALTER IOOSS JR. (OPPOSITE)

OCTOBER 24 ›

Josh Beckett dominates
Colorado in Game 1 of the World Series; the Red Sox put up a 7 on the Fenway scoreboard in the fifth inning and pound the Rockies 13-1

OCTOBER 25 ›

Mike Lowell hits a
fifth-inning double to drive in David Ortiz with what would be the winning run. Three days later, Lowell, an unlikely hero, is named World Series MVP

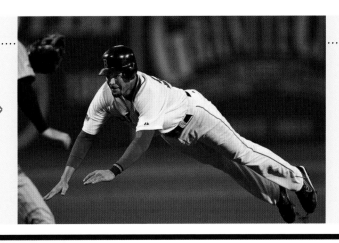

OCTOBER 25

Jonathan Papelbon
strikes out the Rockies' Brian Hawpe to end the game and secure a 2-1 Boston victory in Game 2. The Sox will win the next two games in Colorado, completing a Series sweep

FENWAY PARK   AME

P		1	2	3	4	5	6	7	8	9	H	R	H	E		P	
27	KC	0	0	0	0	0	0	0	0	0		0	0	1		TEX
31	BOSTON	0	0	5	0	0	2	0				7	5	1		MIN
																TO
AT BAT BALL STRI																OAK

13

2008

›››››

...U.S. CONGRESS CONDUCTS
BAILOUT OF SOME OF NATION'S
LARGEST FINANCIAL INSTITUTIONS
...CELTICS WIN A 17TH NBA
CHAMPIONSHIP...NASA CONFIRMS
ICE ON MARS...

‹ **APRIL 3**

A red-tailed hawk attacks
13-year-old Alexa Rodriguez during
a student tour of Fenway. She is
taken away by ambulance but has
only a small cut on her scalp

APRIL 8 ›

Steven Tyler, of the Boston band
Aerosmith, leads the crowd in
singing *God Bless America* during
the seventh-inning stretch

^

MAY 19

When Jon Lester throws
a no-hitter, the catcher
is Jason Varitek; it is the
fourth career no-hitter
caught by Varitek,
a major league record

WINSLOW TOWNSON/AP; JIM ROGASH/GETTY IMAGES (OPPOSITE)

JUNE 20 >

The Celtics' Paul Pierce
shows off the NBA title
trophy won three days
earlier when Boston beat
the L.A. Lakers

SEPTEMBER 8

Pitcher Tim Wakefield
greets fans arriving for the
456th consecutive sellout at
Fenway, an MLB record

2009

>>>>>>

*. . . BARACK OBAMA SWORN IN
AS U.S. PRESIDENT . . . MICHAEL
JACKSON DIES . . . ROGER FEDERER
WINS FRENCH OPEN, THEN
WIMBLEDON FOR RECORD 15TH
MAJOR TITLE . . .*

APRIL 26

Jacoby Ellsbury steals home in
the fifth inning against the
Yankees, the first steal of home by
a Red Sox player in 10 years

AUGUST 28

Architect Janet Marie Smith, who
presided over the multiyear renovation of
Fenway to accolades, leaves her position

2010

›››››

...BP OILWELL EXPLODES OFF
LOUISIANA COAST...BOSTON
COLLEGE WINS FROZEN FOUR,
ITS THIRD TITLE OF THE DECADE
...JAZZ BASSIST ESPERANZA
SPALDING UPSETS JUSTIN
BIEBER TO WIN GRAMMY FOR
BEST NEW ARTIST...

JANUARY 1

The NHL Winter Classic
is played before 38,112
fans who watch the Bruins
beat the Philadelphia
Flyers 2-1 in OT

‹ JUNE 9

A bronze statue of Ted Williams,
Bobby Doerr, Johnny Pesky and Dom
DiMaggio, commemorating David
Halberstam's book *The Teammates:
Portrait of a Friendship*, is unveiled
near Gate B. An earlier statue of
Williams handing his cap to a small
boy, is relocated nearby

BRIAN SNYDER/REUTERS; DAMIAN STROHMEYER (OPPOSITE)

JULY 21

In the first soccer match played at Fenway in 42 years, Celtic FC of Scotland defeats Sporting CP of Portugal

SEPTEMBER 14

The Boston premiere of The Town, a film shot in part at Fenway a year earlier with Ben Affleck and Jeremy Renner, is celebrated with a cast appearance on the Fenway turf. The movie opens nationally three days later

SEPTEMBER 17

Dark for two months of repairs, the Citgo sign, with 218,000 new LED lights, is relit for the seventh-inning stretch

DAMIAN STROHMEYER (2)

2011

›››››

...LONGTIME BOSTON FUGITIVE JAMES (WHITEY) BULGER IS ARRESTED IN SANTA MONICA, CALIF... AFTER 25 YEARS, "THE OPRAH WINFREY SHOW" AIRS ITS FINALE... THE BRUINS BECOME THE FOURTH BOSTON PRO TEAM IN A SPAN OF SEVEN YEARS TO WIN A CHAMPIONSHIP; BEANTOWN IS TITLETOWN...

‹ APRIL 8

At the beginning of Fenway's 100th season, a massive Diamond Vision scoreboard is unveiled, marking the completion of the park's 10-year renovation project

ʌ
APRIL 9

New first baseman Adrian Gonzalez shows his skills in the opening series against New York. Gonzalez will finish the year leading the team in batting average (.338) and RBIs (117)

ʌ
MAY 21

The Chicago Cubs visit Fenway for the first time since 1918. To honor the occasion, the Red Sox go retro, with 1918 uniforms

˅

AUGUST 15

Sox second baseman, fan favorite Dustin Pedroia, is on the cover of SPORTS ILLUSTRATED. Despite a splendid season, he is not able to lift the Red Sox back to the playoffs

AUGUST 31

In his 15th season, all with the Red Sox, catcher Jason Varitek hits a two-run 8th-inning homer to help beat the Yankees and further secure his place in Fenway history

SEPTEMBER 13

Knuckleballer Tim Wakefield, in his 17th season with Boston, gets his 200th win, beating Toronto. "I've always said I've been grateful to wear this uniform," he says

2012 AND BEYOND

A much longer life for Fenway Park is now virtually assured by its current caretakers. And while David Ortiz won't be around for too many more years, who knows—perhaps sometime around 2030 his son D'Angelo (Little Papi?) will be banging balls off the enduring and beloved Fenway wall

FACSIMILE

If imitation is the sincerest form of flattery, then no ballpark is as beloved as Fenway, which has spawned a host of inspired re-creations

HOME TO WIFFLE BALL players in Jericho, Vt., this faux Fenway, built by Patrick O'Connor and friends, comes complete with all the iconic trappings—including the Citgo sign and retired numbers.

Photograph by PETER GREGOIRE

∧ **IN MAINE, THE PORTLAND**
Sea Dogs, a Double A affiliate
of the Red Sox, get prepared
for the real Fenway by playing
in their own smaller version.
Photograph by ROBERT F. BUKATY

< **A LEGO CONSTRUCTION OF**
Fenway Park, built to scale
with precise dimensions,
can't be played in, but can
certainly be admired.
Photograph by PATRICK HANEY

∧ **IT'S OPENING DAY, WITH FULL** pomp and pageantry, at the Fenway in Westfield, Mass., a beautifully detailed park (note the netting) in the backyard of Chris and Jen Dolan

Photograph by SCOTT M. BOIS

OF ALL PEOPLE, THE VILIFIED BUCKY > Dent is proprietor of his own Fenway at his baseball school in Delray Beach, Fla. His young charges clearly root not for Dent's Yankees, but Fenway's Sox.

Photograph by BILL FRAKES

FORMER RED SOX CENTERFIELDER >> Fred Lynn is right at home in front of the Green Monster lovingly built by displaced Sox fan George O'Donnell in his backyard in Clackamas, Ore.

Photograph by GREG WALL-STEPHENS

THE FENWAY 100: FAVORITE FACTOIDS

From a century's worth of historical tidbits about Fenway Park, these are the best

100 THE FIRST EVENT HELD AT FENWAY PARK WAS AN exhibition game between the Red Sox and Harvard; it was played in a snowstorm. The big leaguers won 2–0.

99 THERE HAVE BEEN 11,387 HOME RUNS HIT AT FENWAY, THE first by Sox first baseman Hugh Bradley six days after it opened.

98 IN THE BOTTOM OF THE NINTH OF AN AUGUST 2002 GAME, pinch runner Rickey Henderson stole second, the last of his American League record 1,270 swipes. He stole 51 bases in 60 attempts at Fenway.

97 THE MASSACHUSETTS SUPREME COURT RULED AGAINST Mrs. Lillian Shaw in her suit to receive $25,000 in damages for a broken jaw she suffered in Fenway on April 26, 1942, the result of a foul ball hit by Yankees catcher Buddy Rosar. In a landmark decision for baseball, the court ruled that being hit by a foul ball is a risk that the spectator knowingly assumes when attending a game.

96 BOSTON REDSKINS TACKLE GLENN EDWARDS DECIDED the first NFL football game at Fenway by blocking a Giants extra-point attempt in a 21–20 win over New York.

95 MORE THAN 40,000 PACKED FENWAY ON JUNE 11, 1934 TO celebrate the career of Cardinal William O'Connell.

94 MORE THAN 50,000 PACKED FENWAY ON JUNE 10, 1945, FOR a prayer service led by Archbishop Richard J. Cushing

93 NEW GROUND RULES HAD TO BE QUICKLY INSTALLED IN the 1912 American League opener at Fenway when thousands of fans spilled into the outfield before the first pitch against the visiting New York Highlanders. The area was roped off and officials declared that any ball landing among the fans would be ruled a double.

92 DETROIT'S WILLIE HORTON, IN A GAME ON APRIL 14, 1974, HIT a foul popup that struck and killed a pigeon.

91 THE AFL'S FIRST GAME AT FENWAY WAS A 20–14 BOSTON Patriots win over the Oakland Raiders on Oct. 11, 1963. The Pats had played their opener at BC's Alumni Stadium and were not allowed to play at their Fenway home until the Red Sox completed their season.

90 RED SOX STARTER BILLY ROHR PITCHED A ONE-HIT SHUTOUT win in his major league debut at Fenway on April 14, 1967. In the next two seasons, he would win only twice more and by the winter of '68 was out of baseball.

89 WINSLOW KARLSON, A FORMER BASKETBALL PLAYER WHO once played with Jim Thorpe, worked for the Red Sox in some capacity continuously for 66 years, from 1906 through '72. Karlson spent the final 20 years of his life taking tickets, under the leftfield grandstands.

88 THE GAME ON MAY 17, 1947, WAS INTERRUPTED WHEN a seagull dropped a smelt on the mound near St. Louis Browns pitcher Ellis Kinder; he picked up the fish by the tail, delivered it to the dugout, then returned to the mound to finish his day with a 4–2 win.

87 NO PLAYER, INCLUDING RED SOX, HAS A HIGHER CAREER slugging percentage at Fenway than Frank Robinson's .724, with 157 total bases in 217 at bats.

86 THE FIRST NO-HITTER THROWN AT FENWAY PARK WAS BY Boston but not the Red Sox. It was Boston Braves hurler George Davis who blanked the Phillies 7–0 in 1914.

85 WASHINGTON RELIEF PITCHER ELMER SINGLETON WAS the winning pitcher in a 1950 game in which he gave up a hit on the one pitch he threw. Boston's Vern Stephens drove in Johnny Pesky and Dom DiMaggio with a single on Singleton's lone pitch, tying the game at 7–7, but Stephens was thrown out at second to end the sixth inning. Washington scored twice in the top of the seventh to give Singleton the W.

84 IN 1950 THE RED SOX HELD AN ILL-FATED "CADDY DAY" AT Fenway, handing out golf balls to fans. When the Red Sox lost the game, balls pelted the field like hailstones.

83 RED SOX THIRD BASEMAN JOHN KRONER WAS THE FIRST player to hit a home run into the 23' 7" high net attached to the top of Fenway Park's leftfield wall during the summer of 1936.

82 TED WILLIAMS, OFTEN BOOED AS A PLAYER, WAS GREETED by a big Fenway crowd in 1969 with a long standing ovation upon making his return to Fenway as the manager of the Washington Senators.

81 RIGHTFIELDER TONY CONIGLIARO AND BROTHER BILLY, also an outfielder, teamed up to hit 54 home runs in 1970, the most in major league history by two relatives on the same team.

80 KNOWN AS "THE MAN WITH THE MEGAPHONE," JOHN J. Sweeney, of Woonsocket, R.I., was perhaps Boston's most recognizable fan during the first five decades at Fenway. Never shy in his opinions, Sweeney always used his megaphone for emphasis.

79 WHEN REGGIE JACKSON LOAFED AFTER A BALL IN THE outfield in a June 18, 1977 game, Yankees manager Billy Martin sent outfielder Paul Blair out to replace him, mid-inning. Humiliated, Jackson got into a nasty screaming match with Martin on the dugout steps—and on national TV.

78 IN THE FIRST COLLEGE FOOTBALL GAME AT FENWAY PARK, in 1914, the Boston College Eagles beat the Norwich Cadets 28–6.

77 IN A FENWAY EXHIBITION DURING HIS MARINES DUTY, TED Williams took on Babe Ruth in a 1943 home run hitting contest. The aging and noticeably limping Babe Ruth was unable to put a ball over the fence; the youthful Williams delivered, even depositing a Ruthian blast into the unoccupied centerfield bleachers.

76 ON OPENING DAY 1924, IN WHAT MAY BE THE MOST inauspicious Red Sox debut ever, shortstop Bill Wambsganss, traded to Boston after a long career in Cleveland, booted two ninth-inning ground balls, allowing the Yankees to score two runs and win 2–1.

75 IN 77 GAMES AT FENWAY PARK, MINNESOTA'S TONY OLIVA hit .376 (121 for 322), the highest career batting average for anyone with at least 300 at bats at Fenway. The Red Sox career batting average leader at Fenway is Wade Boggs at .369

74 IN 1921 RED SOX FIRST BASEMAN STUFFY McINNIS COMMITTED just one error all season—and none at Fenway—in 1,652 chances, setting a major league record for fielding percentage for an infielder.

73 NEW YORK GIANTS CENTERFIELDER FRED SNODGRASS famously blundered when he dropped an easy fly ball hit by Boston's Clyde Engle in the 10th inning to ignite a two-run rally and give the Red Sox a come-from-behind win in the deciding Game 8 of the 1912 World Series.

72 BOBBY DOERR IS THE ONLY PLAYER TO HAVE HIT FOR THE cycle twice at Fenway. Fifteen men—10 Red Sox and five visitors—have managed the feat; Bengie Molina of the Rangers in 2010 being the most recent. The last Boston player to complete the circuit was John Valentin in '96.

71 THE 1933 CHICAGO BEARS LOST 10–0 TO THE BOSTON REDSKINS at Fenway despite playing five future Pro Football Hall of Famers: Red Grange, Bronko Nagurski, Bill Hewitt, Link Lyman and George Musso.

70 BOSTON CATCHER SCOTT HATTEBERG, IN A 2001 GAME against the Rangers, hit into a triple play in the fourth inning. Two innings later he hit a grand slam. He remains the only player in modern baseball history to do both in the same game.

69 DURING THE SEVENTH INNING OF A SOX-MARINERS GAME in 1983, Boston police entered the home dugout and arrested Red Sox infielder Julio Valdez on charges of statutory rape of a 14-year-old girl; he was led from the clubhouse in handcuffs. Valdez was never indicted.

68 BUCKY DENT'S GO-AHEAD THREE-RUN HOME RUN IN THE 1978 Red Sox–Yankees one-game playoff went down in history as a shocker; but the light-hitting shortstop had in fact enjoyed great success at Fenway that summer, driving in 12 runs—more than any visiting AL hitter in '78, two more than teammate Reggie Jackson's 10.

67 IN 1924, AREA BOY SCOUTS DREW 20,000 SPECTATORS TO Fenway to see demonstrations of such skills as fire-starting and semaphore flag signaling.

66 FENWAY PARK WAS SUPPOSED TO HOST THE 1945 ALL-STAR Game but it was canceled due to World War II. The game was played at Fenway in 1946; the AL won 12–0 as Ted Williams had two homers and five RBIs. Fenway was the last of the AL's eight parks to host the game.

65 DURING A GAME ON MAY 26, 1946, AFTER A WIND SHIFT, THE temperature dropped in a matter of minutes from 83° to 58°.

64 THE FIRST BROTHERS TO PLAY IN THE SAME GAME IN FENWAY as Red Sox were starting catcher Alex Gaston and his brother Milt, who came in to pitch a scoreless seventh inning against the Browns in 1929.

63 WHEN THE BAND PHISH PLAYED FENWAY AS PART OF THEIR 2009 reunion tour, they opened the show by singing *The Star-Spangled Banner* from the pitchers mound while wearing Red Sox jerseys.

62 MICKEY MANTLE AND BABE RUTH EACH HIT 38 HOME RUNS as visiting players at Fenway Park, the most for any Red Sox opponent. (Harmon Killebrew was one behind with 37.) Ruth also hit the first home run by a visiting player over the new 37-foot wall in leftfield in 1934.

61 MICKEY MANTLE STRUCK OUT MORE TIMES AT FENWAY than any opposing player, 134 times in 644 plate appearances.

60 A KEY REASON WHY OWNER GEORGE PRESTON MARSHALL moved his Redskins from Boston to Washington in 1937 was the popularity of their Fenway co-tenants, the AFL's best team, the Boston Shamrocks. However the Shamrocks proceeded to cease operations after the '37 season.

59 IN 1952, ON A SPECIAL DAY TO HONOR HIM BEFORE HE returned to the Marine Corps to fight in Korea, Ted Williams hit a game-winning home run against the Tigers.

58 FROM MAY 30, 1924 UNTIL THE FIRST TWO GAMES OF THE '36 season, the Red Sox never held first place on consecutive home dates.

57 TWO OF THE EIGHT UNASSISTED TRIPLE PLAYS IN AL history happened at Fenway: by Sox first baseman George Burns in 1923 and by Sox shortstop John Valentin in '94

56 TRAILING THE ANGELS BY A RUN IN THE 11TH INNING ON June 8, 1961, Boston centerfielder Gary Geiger hit a triple to drive in Chuck Schilling with what Geiger thought was the winning run; but it only tied the score at 4–4. After reaching third Geiger continued on into the Red Sox clubhouse and was called out. The game would end in a tie due to the AL curfew.

55 ROGER CLEMENS MADE EXACTLY 200 STARTS AT FENWAY IN his career, earning wins in exactly 100.

54 AS A VISITING PITCHER AT FENWAY, ROGER CLEMENS NEVER had a loss, going 5–0.

53 THE MOST RUNS EVER SCORED BY A TEAM IN FENWAY PARK was 29 by the Red Sox in a 29–4 win over the St. Louis Browns in 1950.

52 TED WILLIAMS, AN AVID HUNTER, WAS KNOWN TO SHOOT pigeons inside Fenway; that drew the scrutiny of the Massachusetts SPCA, but he was never "caught" in the act.

51 FEWER THAN 500 PEOPLE SHOWED UP AT FENWAY FOR BACK-to-back games in 1965 against the Angels: on Sept. 28 (461) and Sept. 29 (409).

50 IN 100 YEARS, JUST THREE RED SOX PLAYERS HAVE HOMERED in their first major league at bat: Daniel Nava (2010), Eddie Pellagrini (1946) and Lefty LeFebvre (1938). All three did it at Fenway.

49 LEGENDARY FOOTBALL COACHES COL. ROBERT NEYLAND and George Halas squared off in a 1942 exhibition game at Fenway between an Army all-star team and the Chicago Bears. In what had seemed a mismatch, Neyland's makeshift military unit frustrated Halas's powerful Bears before Chicago finally pulled out a 14–7 win.

48 ON JUNE 19, 1991, THE RED SOX ISSUED A STATEMENT condemning a nude anatomically correct inflatable doll that had become a regular visitor to Fenway and was passed around among fans.

47 THE ONLY NHL GAME EVER PLAYED IN FENWAY RESULTED in an overtime thriller with Bruin Marco Sturm scoring 1:57 into overtime to give the B's a 2–1 win over the visiting Philadelphia Flyers in the NHL's 2010 Winter Classic.

46 DURING HIS CAREER TED WILLIAMS HAD THREE WALK-off home runs at Fenway—all three of them came against the Detroit Tigers.

45 WHEN EARL WILSON NO-HIT THE L.A. ANGELS ON JUNE 26, 1962, he drove in the only run he needed with a solo homer.

44 ST. LOUIS BROWNS OUTFIELDER BOB NIEMAN SET A MAJOR league record, never matched, by hitting home runs in his first two big league at bats on Sept. 14, 1951. Both cleared the Green Monster.

43 THE RED SOX ESCAPED A LOSS IN A JULY 14, 1916 GAME WHEN Browns base runner Ernie Koob, a pitcher, missed third while attempting to score the first run of a scoreless game in the 15th inning. The contest ended in a 17-inning 0–0 tie. The unfortunate Koob pitched the whole way.

42 AS A BLUE JAY IN 2000, PITCHER DAVID WELLS SAID OF FENWAY, "When they want someone to push the button, I want to be the guy to blow this place up." His disaffection seemed misplaced; Wells's career record at Fenway: 20–13.

41 THE LONGEST GAME EVER PLAYED AT FENWAY WAS A 20-inning contest on Sept. 3, 1981 against the Mariners. The game was suspended after 19 innings due to the 1 a.m. American League curfew and finished the following day with an 8–7 Boston loss.

40 THE LARGEST BASEBALL CROWD IN FENWAY PARK HISTORY was 47,627, for a doubleheader with the Yankees in September 1935. Some 5,000 fans watched from a roped-off section created in deep rightfield.

39 FROM 1944 TO 1998, ELIZABETH DOOLEY OF BOSTON attended more than 4,000 consecutive Sox home games, always in her same seat: first row, Box 36-A. Dooley, who was one year younger than Fenway Park, died in 2000.

38 THE BOSTON YANKS PULLED OFF A STUNNING 37–14 UPSET over the eventual NFL champion Philadelphia Eagles in the team's final game at Fenway, on Dec. 5, 1948. The Yanks, 3–9 for the year, then folded.

37 ONLY ONE VISITING PLAYER HAS HAD AT LEAST 200 HITS AT Fenway Park, Detroit's Al Kaline with 218. (Luke Appling had 199.)

36 ON JULY 15, 1967, ORIOLES CENTERFIELDER PAUL BLAIR HIT into a triple play on the first swing of the game. After the first two batters had walked without swinging, Blair followed with a line drive to Boston third baseman Joe Foy who started an around-the-horn triple play.

35 ACCORDING TO A 1999 REPORT BY C.H. JOHNSON CONSULTING Inc., "[Tourism statistics] indicate that Fenway Park attracts more visitors to Boston than any other single attraction."

34 CARL EVERETT IS THE ONLY PLAYER TO HIT HOME RUNS IN six straight games at Fenway, between June 25 and July 16, 2000.

33 PITCHER AND FREE-SPIRIT BILL (SPACEMAN) LEE, UPON seeing the Green Monster for the first time in 1969, said, "Do they leave it up there during games?"

32 LOU GEHRIG DROVE IN 150 RUNS AT FENWAY, BESTING ANY other visiting player by far. Babe Ruth is a distant second with 119.

31 THE LAST CAMPAIGN SPEECH OF PRESIDENT FRANKLIN D. Roosevelt's career on Nov. 4, 1944, was given at Fenway Park. He won reelection to his fourth and final term three days later.

30 AFTER A MAY 1926 FIRE BURNED DOWN THE LEFTFIELD stands, a gaping void was left, thus creating the largest foul territory in big league history; during the time the empty foul space remained, the batting average for all players at Fenway went down by 10 points.

29 WHEN JACOBY ELLSBURY DROPPED A LINE DRIVE TO DEEP center off the bat of Florida's Jorge Cantu on June 17, 2009, it was the first error of his major league career, a span of 232 games.

28 ON JUNE 9, 1931, CLUB OWNER BOB QUINN REJECTED A proposal by the Shortwave and Television Corp. to televise Red Sox games from Fenway. Wrote Quinn in a wire, "It has rained every Sunday, our club is in last place and now you want me to let them see the game at home? If you furnish me with a substitute for money, please let me know immediately."

27 AT THE 1999 ALL-STAR GAME AT FENWAY, BOSTON'S PEDRO Martinez retired all six batters he faced, five by strikeout.

26 THE FIRST ROCK CONCERT IN THE 91-YEAR HISTORY OF Fenway Park history was performed by Bruce Springsteen and the E Street Band in 2003. Citing the Curse of the Bambino, he invoked a "rock 'n' roll exorcism." A year later the curse would be broken.

25 THE RED SOX PLAYED NO SUNDAY GAMES AT FENWAY before 1932 because the park stood within 850 feet of the Church of the Disciples; city law prohibited baseball from being played within 1,000 feet of a church on Sundays. In May of '32, the church relented to a statute changing the distance from 1,000 feet to 700.

24 IN 2005 DAVID ORTIZ SCORED A RUN IN 19 STRAIGHT GAMES at Fenway, shattering the mark of 15 set in 1950 by Billy Goodman.

23 IN 1945, JACKIE ROBINSON RECEIVED A TRYOUT IN FENWAY and hit impressively. Red Sox management, however, decided to pass.

22 ON AUG. 15, 1922 THE RED SOX AND WHITE SOX COMBINED for an AL record 36 singles, 21 by Chicago and 15 by Boston.

21 JUST 15,238 FANS ATTENDED THE CLINCHING GAME OF THE 1918 World Series, a backlash to the earlier threat that Game 4 wouldn't be played due to a player strike over gate receipts.

20 THE FIRST OPEN AIR BOXING CARD IN FENWAY'S HISTORY, IN 1920, was marred by an brawl between heavyweights John Lester Johnson and Battling McCreery. After a 10-round decision for McCreery, Johnson slugged the winner during the postfight handshake. McCreery proceeded to knock Johnson through the ropes and hit him with a chair.

19 JUST TWO DAYS AFTER HIS CONTRACT WAS PURCHASED FROM the minor-league Baltimore Orioles on July 9, 1914, 19-year old George Ruth pitched six innings of scoreless ball before surrendering two runs to the Cleveland Naps. (The Babe would go 0-for-2 at the plate.)

18 THERE HAVE BEEN 49 INSIDE-THE-PARK HOME RUNS BY RED Sox players at Fenway; Tris Speaker hit eight of them in 1912 alone.

17 A JULY 1973 MUSIC FESTIVAL, FEATURING RAY CHARLES, Stevie Wonder and B.B. King, turned ugly when singer Donnie Hathaway took the stage and patrons surged onto the field. Fans jumped atop the dugouts; onlookers were shoved, threatened, even robbed. Fenway didn't host another concert for three decades.

16 IN A 1986 GAME, ROGER CLEMENS STRUCK OUT 20 SEATTLE Mariners to set the modern major league record.

15 RON BLOMBERG OF THE YANKEES BECAME THE FIRST designated hitter to bat in American League history on April 6, 1973 at Fenway when he walked with the bases loaded against Boston's Luis Tiant.

14 LARRY GARDNER, A RED SOX THIRD BASEMAN FROM 1908 through '17, learned early about the vagaries of the Wall in leftfield. As he described it afterward, "I stood at the plate watching a long foul to left. The wind blew it fair against the fence. They threw me out at first."

13 BETWEEN MAY 3, 1938 AND JUNE 21, 1941 BOSTON'S LEFTY Grove won 20 straight decisions at Fenway, easily the longest stretch of success there for any pitcher. (The second longest such streak is 14.)

12 IN 28 GAMES AS A VISITING PITCHER TO FENWAY DURING his career, Lefty Grove went 16–5.

11 NOT ONLY WAS BABE RUTH SOLD TO THE YANKEES FOR $100,000 in 1919 but Red Sox owner Harry Frazee also secured a $300,000 mortgage loan from Yanks owner Col. Jacob Ruppert, with Fenway Park itself as collateral.

10 THE FIRST CROWD OF OVER 50,000 AT FENWAY PARK WAS comprised mainly of schoolchildren who, in the summer of 1914, cheered a trio of elephants, Mollie, Tony and Waddy, before the pachyderms took up permanent residence in the Franklin Park Zoo.

9 THERE HAVE BEEN 13 NO-HITTERS THROWN AT FENWAY PARK. There has never been a perfect game thrown there.

8 THE FIRST FOUR NUMBERS RETIRED AT FENWAY WERE FOR TED Williams (9), Joe Cronin (4), Bobby Doerr (1) and Carl Yastrzemski (8). They were originally placed on the rightfield facade in chronological order of when the numbers were retired, until someone noted that 9/4/18 was the day before the start of what was then the last World Series won by the Red Sox. In the late '90s they were rearranged in numeric order.

7 A RED SEAT IN RIGHTFIELD MARKS THE LANDING SPOT OF the longest home run in Fenway history, a 1946 blast by Ted Williams measuring 502 feet. In 2001 Manny Ramirez hit a massive clout of his own over the Green Monster that was measured at, curiously enough, 501 feet.

6 AFTER TAKING A CALLED THIRD STRIKE IN A 1958 GAME, TED Williams angrily flung his bat, which flew into the box seats and happened to hit the 75-year-old housekeeper of former Sox manager Joe Cronin. As she was being carried from the seats for a trip to the hospital, she said, "Why are they booing Ted?"

5 THE ONLY MAN TO PLAY FOR THE RED SOX, BRUINS AND CELTICS? John Kiley, who played the organ at Fenway from 1953 to '89 and at the Boston Garden from 1942 to '84.

4 IN THE FIRST INNING ON JUNE 23, 1917 RED SOX STARTER BABE Ruth's first three pitches were balls and already he was fuming at umpire Brick Owen. When the ump called ball four, Ruth stalked to the plate as Owen removed his mask and came out to meet him. Ruth hit Owen with a looping right hand punch and was ejected. Ernie Shore entered the game in relief. On Shore's first pitch, the Washington base runner, Ray Morgan, was thrown out trying to steal second. Shore set down the next 26 batters for a "near perfect" game.

3 THOMAS YAWKEY SPENT THE SAME AMOUNT ON RENOVATIONS to Fenway ($1.5 million) in 1934 as he did to purchase the park and the team.

2 CARL YASTRZEMSKI IS THE LAST PLAYER TO WIN BASEBALL'S Triple Crown. To do it, Yaz went 7 for 8 at Fenway against the Twins in the last two games of '67 to raise his final average to a league-leading .326.

1 TED WILLIAMS, AS ALL BOSTON FANS KNOW, HIT A HOME RUN IN his final Red Sox at bat, in Fenway on Sept. 28, 1960. But Boston still had three road games to play in New York. Williams went fishing instead.

ACKNOWLEDGMENTS

EXPLORING A CENTURY'S WORTH OF history requires long days of inspired effort, in this case inspired by the allure of Fenway Park itself. This book is indebted to these dedicated members of the SPORTS ILLUSTRATED staff: Geoff Michaud, Dan Larkin, Bob Thompson, Damian Strohmeyer, Karen Carpenter, Prem Kalliat, George Amores, Joe Felice, Will Welt, Steve Fine, Nate Gordon, Erick Rasco, Don Delliquanti, Michael Cummo, Chris Hercik, Jay Soysal, Dwayne Bernard, Liana Zamora, Tracy Mothershed, Joy Birdsong, Dick Friedman, Kostya Kennedy, MJ Day, Leon Avelino and Linda Verigan as well as Time Inc. Sports Group Editor Terry McDonell. Thanks also to Parker Day, Drew Kaufman and Lillibelle Rasco.

Special thanks for their generous help goes to Tom Blake and Jane Winton at the Boston Public Library, Bob Cullum, Winslow Townson, Mike Raphael, Bev Wilson at The Topps Company, Inc., Pat Kelly at the National Baseball Hall of Fame, and Dick Bresciani and Michael Ivins of the Boston Red Sox.

These pages are filled with the contributions of the exceptional photographers and writers of SI, past and present; an admiring thank you goes out to all of those whose brilliant work appears in this book.

Grateful acknowledgment is also made to the following for permission to reprint copyrighted material:

All You Ever Wanted in a Ball Park—and Less Copyright © 1975 by Melvin Maddocks. Used by permission of the estate of Melvin Maddocks.

Babe: The Legend Comes to Life Copyright © 1974 by Robert W. Creamer. Copyright renewed © 2002 by Robert W. Creamer. Used by permission of Simon & Schuster Inc.

Plink-Rumba-Barumba-Boom Copyright © 1993 by Roy Blount Jr.

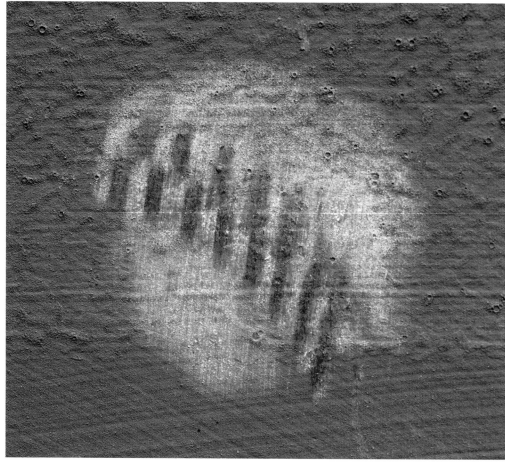

DAMIAN STROHMEYER

The Green Monster is tattooed with marks made when batted balls strike the wall.

Historic artifacts used courtesy of the National Baseball Hall of Fame. Topps baseball cards used courtesy of The Topps Company, Inc.

COVER: FRONT (left to right, from top): Erick W. Rasco, Chuck Solomon, The Brearley Collection, Clay Patrick McBride, Harry Cabluck/AP, David E. Klutho, Focus on Sport/Getty Images. **BACK** (left to right, from top): Erick W. Rasco, Boston Public Library, John Biever, Kevin Mazur/Wireimage.com, Bettmann/Corbis (2). **FRONT FLAP:** National Baseball Hall of Fame. **BACK FLAP:** Jean-Pierre Lescourret/Corbis.

PICTURES: Corbis: 2–3; Time Life Pictures/Getty Images: 4; Getty Images: 20–23, 48; Boston Public Library Prints: 30, 40–41; The Sporting News/Getty Images: 36–37; Zuma Press: 38; AP: 42, 46–47, 49, 192, 193; Icon SMI: 43; Reuters: 51.

TIMELINE OPENER (left to right, from top): National Baseball Hall of Fame, Leslie Jones Collection/Boston Public Library Prints (3), James F. Coyne, Neil Leifer, Heinz Kluetmeier, Chuck Solomon, Heinz Kluetmeier, Chuck Solomon.

1912–1919 (left to right): Courtesy of Logue Engineering, Library of Congress, National Baseball Hall of Fame, Transcendental Graphics, National Baseball Hall of Fame, Boston Public Library Prints, National Baseball Hall of Fame, Bettmann/Corbis, David N. Berkwitz, Corbis, Underwood & Underwood/Corbis, Boston Public Library Prints, National Baseball Hall of Fame/AP, Underwood & Underwood/Corbis, Boston Public Library, Bettmann/Corbis.

1920–1929 (left to right): Bettmann/Corbis, Transcendental Graphics/Getty Images, Bettmann/Corbis, Boston Public Library Print Department, Corbis, Underwood & Underwood/Corbis, National Baseball Hall of Fame, Bettmann/Corbis, David N. Berkwitz, Walter Iooss Jr., National Baseball Hall of Fame/MLB Photos/Getty Images, Underwood & Underwood/Corbis, Bettmann/Corbis, National Baseball Hall of Fame, Leslie Jones Collection/Boston Public Library Prints.

1930–1939 (left to right): AP, National Baseball Hall of Fame, Boston Public Library Prints, AP, Fox Photos/Getty Images, Leslie Jones Collection/Boston Public Library Prints, Bettmann/Corbis, Courtesy of Boston Red Sox, Bettmann/Corbis, Boston Public Library, National Baseball Hall of Fame/MLB Photos/Getty Images, Bettmann/Corbis, Leslie Jones Collection/Boston Public Library Prints, New York Times Co./Getty Images, AP.

1940–1949 (left to right): AP, Pro Football Hall of Fame/AP, Dave Pickoff/AP, no credit, Gjon Mili/Time Life Pictures/Getty Images, AP, U.S. Army Signal Corps/Boston Public Library, AP, Universal/Tempsport/Corbis, University of Notre Dame Athletics, Bettmann/Corbis, John J. Lent/AP, Bernard Hoffman/Time Life Pictures/Getty Images, AP, John F. Kennedy Presidential Library and Museum, Bryce Vickmark/Icon SMI, The Sporting News/Zuma Press, National Baseball Hall of Fame, Diamond Images/Getty Images, AP, National Baseball Hall of Fame.

1950–1959 (left to right): AP, Bettmann/Corbis, TSN/Icon SMI, AP, Transcendental Graphics, AP, Harlem Globetrotters International, Inc., Courtesy of The Topps Company, Inc., Bettmann/Corbis, Frank Curtin/AP, Bettmann/Corbis (3), Pam Lockeby/Daytona Beach News Journal/AP, John Springer Collection/Corbis, Marvin Koner/Corbis, AP, Rogers Photo Archive/Getty Images, Imagno/Getty Images.

1960–1969 (left to right): Courtesy of The Topps Company, Inc., Frank Curtin/AP, Hulton-Deutsch Collection/Corbis, Icon SMI, AP (2), Bettmann/Corbis, Tony Tomsic/Getty Images, AP, Neil Leifer, Bettmann/Corbis, Fred Kaplan, Bill Chaplis/AP, AP, Bob Daugherty/AP, Herb Scharfman, Bettmann/Corbis (2), David N. Berkwitz, Walter Iooss Jr., Tony Triolo, Dick Raphael, Courtesy of The Boston Globe, Erick W. Rasco.

1970–1979 (left to right): Bettmann/Corbis, James Drake, Bettmann/Corbis, Courtesy of The Topps Company, Inc., AP, David Reed/Redferns/Getty Images, Long Photography, Dick Raphael, AP, Ken Regan/Camera 5 (2), AP, John Iacono, Harry Cabluck/AP, AP (2), TSN/Zuma Press/Icon SMI, James Drake, Manny Millan, AP (2), Heinz Kluetmeier (2), Bettmann/Corbis, AP.

1980–1989 (left to right): Diamond Images/Getty Images, Rich Pilling/MLB Photos/Getty Images, Courtesy of The Topps Company, Inc., Ted Gartland/The Boston Herald/AP, Bettmann/Corbis, Paul Benoit/AP, Courtesy of NESN, Dave Tenenbaum/AP, John D. Hanlon, Chuck Solomon, John D. Hanlon, John Iacono, Therese Frare/AP, Steve Lipofsky/Corbis.

1990–1999 (left to right): College Baseball Daily, Keith Torrie/New York Daily News Archive/Getty Images, Heinz Kluetmeier, John Iacono, Manny Millan, Jon Chase/AP, Time Life Pictures/Getty Images, Scott Maguire/AP, Damian Strohmeyer (2), Charles Krupa/AP, Steven Senne/AP, Elise Amendola/AP, Jim Rogash/AP, Damian Strohmeyer, Charles Krupa/AP, The Boston Preservation Alliance and Save Fenway, Inc., Damian Strohmeyer (2).

2000–2011 (left to right): K.C. Bailey/American Broadcasting Companies, Inc., Steven Senne/AP, Elsa/Getty Images, Brian Snyder/Reuters, Mike Mergen/AP, Elise Amendola/AP, Neal Hamberg/AP, Jim Bourg/Reuters, Rhona Wise/Icon SMI, Brian Snyder/Reuters/Corbis, Jim Rogash/Wireimage.com, John Iacono, Damian Strohmeyer, Chuck Solomon, Al Tielemans, Robert Silvers/photomosaic.com, Milo Stewart/National Baseball Hall of Fame, Damian Strohmeyer, Neal Hamberg/Reuters (2), Charles Krupa/AP, Robert E. Klein/AP, Elise Amendola/AP, Matt Campbell/EPA, Chuck Solomon, Al Tielemans, John Tlumacki/Boston Globe/Landov, Steven Senne/AP, Brian Babineau/NBAE/Getty Images, Jim Rogash/Getty Images, Stanley Hu/AP, Steven Senne/AP, Claire Folger/Warner Brothers/The Everett Collection, Winslow Townson/AP, Damian Strohmeyer, David Butler II/US Presswire, Damian Strohmeyer, Adam Hunger/Reuters.

END PAPERS: Damian Strohmeyer (4).

TIME HOME ENTERTAINMENT: Richard Fraiman, PUBLISHER; Steven Sandonato, VICE PRESIDENT, BUSINESS DEVELOPMENT & STRATEGY; Carol Pittard, EXECUTIVE DIRECTOR, MARKETING SERVICES; Tom Mifsud, EXECUTIVE DIRECTOR, RETAIL & SPECIAL SALES; Peter Harper, EXECUTIVE DIRECTOR, NEW PRODUCT DEVELOPMENT; Laura Adam, DIRECTOR, BOOKAZINE DEVELOPMENT & MARKETING; Joy Butts, PUBLISHING DIRECTOR; Glenn Buonocore, FINANCE DIRECTOR; Helen Wan, ASSISTANT GENERAL COUNSEL; Ilene Schreider, ASSISTANT DIRECTOR, SPECIAL SALES; Anne-Michelle Gallero, DESIGN & PREPRESS MANAGER; Susan Chodakiewicz, BOOK PRODUCTION MANAGER; Allison Parker, BRAND MANAGER; Alex Voznesenskiy, ASSOCIATE PREPRESS MANAGER; Stephen Koepp, EDITORIAL DIRECTOR

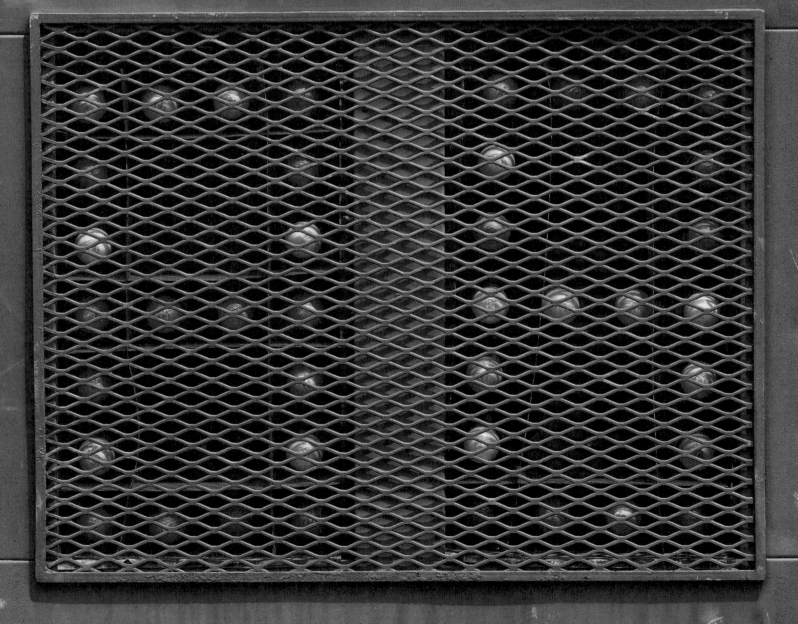